SCRAMBLE
STAYMAN

Doug Bennion

An Honors Book from Master Point Press

Master Point Press
214 Merton St. Suite 205
Toronto, Ontario, Canada
M4S 1A6
(647) 956-4933

info@masterpointpress.com

www.masterpointpress.com
www.bridgeblogging.com
www.teachbridge.com
www.ebooksbridge.com

ISBN: 978-1-77140-160-9

Cover Design: Olena S. Sullivan/New Mediatrix

1 2 3 4 5 6   19 18 17 16

CONTENTS

4

Introduction

Hey pard we seem to be leaving a
lot of 4-4 major fits on the table!

Your Hunch

Partner opens a weak 1NT (12 to 14). You have your usual dreck. Your hand has less than invitational strength, lacks a long biddable suit, has a shape along the lines of 4-3-4-2 or 2-4-5-2 or 3-4-1-5. It might be this hand:

♠   K 7 6 5
♥   Q 10 2
♦   3
♣   K 7 6 4 2

For most experienced weak notrumpers, that's an automatic pass, but as you finger the green card you suspect, and not for the first time, there may be a good chance 1NT is far from optimum. Suppose partner held four spades, like here?

♠   A Q 4 2
♥   K 9
♦   J 9 8 2
♣   Q J 8

♠   K 7 6 5
♥   Q 10 2
♦   3
♣   K 7 6 4 2

On a good day, 4♠ will make, and any spade contract will usually outscore 1NT. Or, partner has opened 1NT with five hearts (your agreement permits) like so:

♠ A Q
♥ K 9 8 7 3
♦ J 9 8
♣ Q J 8

♠ K 7 6 5
♥ Q 10 2
♦ 3
♣ K 7 6 4 2

4♥ has decent play, and some number of hearts will be a big improvement over 1NT.

How about this layout?

♠ A 9
♥ A J 7 4
♦ J 9 8 7
♣ Q J 8

♠ K 7 6 5
♥ Q 10 2
♦ 3
♣ K 7 6 4 2

That heart Moysian (4-3 fit) should have excellent play in 2♥, with a good chance of scoring better than 1NT. I can see a lot of tricks on a cross ruff, or maybe by setting up clubs.

Opener might even have this fortuitous specimen, where you will be very unlucky not to make a spade game.

♠	A Q 4 3 2
♥	K 9
♦	J 9 8
♣	Q J 8

♠	K 7 6 5
♥	Q 10 2
♦	3
♣	K 7 6 4 2

So by sitting for 1NT with that hand, you are surely missing out on some terrific major-suit fits, which generally will play and score better in 2♥ or 2♠ than 1NT. Nonetheless you pass, because *that's what every bridge authority has been telling you to do since the dawn of bridge time. It's conventional bridge wisdom!* The reason? If you ask about majors with Stayman, and partner as usual has the wrong hand, then what are your options? Opposite 12-14 with K765 QT2 3 K7642, you start 2♣ and opener disappoints with 2♦, now what? You're too weak to undertake a 2NT contract (even if you could force partner to pass it). You aren't comfortable with 3♣ as a secondary option, although it won't always be a poor contract. You're not even sure what to do when he rebids 2♥. So you are told not to ask for a major in that position.

Still, you cannot shake your hunch that maybe it is not optimum to routinely sit for 1NT, that with at least some suitable responding hands you should strike out in search of a major-suit fit. Not every search will succeed, but you speculate you will encounter more good than harm.

Unfortunately you have zero facts at your disposal. Nada. Zilch. *You have no idea what trump fits you might find. You don't know how often you will land in those contracts, or how they would score compared to 1NT. You cringe at what 'horrors' might await if you cannot negotiate a major fit.* As far as you know, nobody has taken a thorough look at outcomes for that position. All you have is your uninformed hunch.

This book does two things. For the big picture, we thoroughly parse your hunch by analyzing tens of thousands of deals, and answer the questions raised in the previous paragraphs. Then we illustrate our findings with a *challenge* match. Spoiler: It turns out your hunch was bang on.

The Proposed Solution

We will institute a simple 'scramble' for a major-suit fit. We have called the new routine *Scramble Stayman*, because it begins with 2♣, and works alongside plain vanilla 2♣ Stayman. It happens to incorporate elements of 'Crawling Stayman' (CS), not by design but because CS emerges from the analysis. The holdings for Scramble Stayman come around much more often than they do for CS, because we scramble with many more hand types, and over a much wider range of responder strength. We *deconstruct and validate* CS along the way. If you are not playing at least (54)xx CS, you should very seriously consider it.

Weak notrumpers love the damage which 1NT inflicts on their opponents, but they overlook (or resign themselves to) the degrading of their own part-score bidding.

A common lament for weak notrump fans is this. My 1NT opener pre-empts *three* 'opponents'. As I score up my +90, I note with some satisfaction the opponents seem to be cold for 2♥. We shut them out with our opening 1NT, yeaaah. When the board results are published, I see a few pairs did manage 110 the other way. Alas (once again) my hard-fought +90 is a sub-average result because other pairs our way found their 4-4 spade fit. 2♠ makes easily, and outscores 1NT. The 1NT opener both wins and loses again!

So although opening with an anti-field 1NT range has many benefits, it is frustrating to miss out on better-scoring partial contracts because you pre-empted *yourself*. I wondered if there was some way responder might mitigate. Could we scramble for 8+ major-suit fits and *if not successful, settle into 'acceptable' if not 'good' contracts*? Would landing in the good spots more than compensate for having to settle for less desirable ones? Several questions come to mind.

- ❑ What kind of responder hand is suitable to scramble? Since our primary goal is finding a major-suit fit, surely a 5-4-2-2 hand would qualify, and 3-2-4-4 not, but what about the likes of 4-3-5-1 or 1-4-4-4 or 4-2-5-2 or even 4-3-4-2?
- ❑ What form would the search take? How would it co-exist with regular Stayman?
- ❑ Ultimately, which kinds of contracts will result, and how often? Lacking a major-suit fit, then what? What are the chances of landing in a 'good' spot?
- ❑ Most importantly, overall will the scramble pay off in improved IMP and matchpoint scoring?

The Challenge Match

On a more intimate scale, to better bring to life our big picture analysis, we've prepared a challenge match. Our analysis is very persuasive, but it's edifying to see actual bridge hands play out. The match will serve as confirmation by example.

What do we mean by 'match'? Our broad analysis identified a simple fit-finding algorithm. The bold match challenger scrambles out of 1NT to play wherever those bidding rules take him. The conservative guy sticks to 1NT at 'the other table'. We randomly deal a batch of suitable hands each with double dummy results (similar to tournament or club hand records). The challenger scrambles to the optimum reachable fit, and we compare scores for that contract with scores for 1NT. You need a very large number of hands to squeeze out all randomness, beyond the capability of a challenge match. The analyses in this book use samples of several thousand. However for illustrative purposes in this match, a sampling of 100 random deals should point us in the right direction.

Any really curious/sceptical reader can actually validate for himself, playing his 'personal' challenge match. Reader will need either a commercial double-dummy dealer, or access to a large number of tournament/club hand records, the kind which includes a double dummy analysis of who makes what. Browse those records for suitable deals, determine the scramble contract, and 'play out' the match by comparing scores for the scramble contract with 1NT.

The scramble position arises much more often for weak notrumpers. They open 1NT more frequently (12-14 comes along about twice as often as 15-17, and 11-14 nearly *thrice* as often), and their sub-invitational range is also wider (0 to

10 or so, compared to about 0 to 7, also about twice as frequent). Since the methods I will introduce have greater utility for weaker notrump ranges, much of this book will focus on 12 to 14 in opener, and 8 or 9 in responder.

Strong notrumpers should note the concept works equally well for, say, 15 to 17 opposite 5 or 6.

We would find that *any* responder strength would benefit from a scramble, not just the focus range.

Distribution Descriptions

Throughout the book we use the following distribution descriptions:

- ❑ '4432' represents any hand with four of one suit, four of another, etc.
- ❑ '4-4-3-2' shows specific holdings in spades-hearts-diamonds-clubs.
- ❑ '4-4-xx' shows four spades and four hearts, with any minor-suit holdings.
- ❑ '(42)xx' represents either 4-2-xx or 2-4-xx.
- ❑ '(42)(52)' shows 4-2-5-2 or 4-2-2-5 or 2-4-5-2 or 2-4-2-5.

Qualifying for the Scramble

A scramble initiated by responder will eventually terminate in a *scramble contract*, either 2♥ or 2♠ if we can connect with a major fit, or 3♣ and 3♦ as fallbacks. Under some circumstances responder will pass 2♦, more on this later. We cannot end the scramble with 2NT because responder almost assuredly will be too weak for that contract to be playable (if responder is invitational or better, his 2♣ call will be standard Stayman with 'normal' follow-ups, not the scramble adaptations, see later how the two methods *mesh*).

We are confident (54)xx holdings will scramble to good contracts, but nowhere have seen hard evidence, and we have no idea what is the 'value' of the scramble, how often and to what extent it will pay off. We speculate that 4-4-xx might fare well, but have no proof. We have a hunch that at least some unbalanced hands with a four-card major will benefit, but could be wrong. And we're totally clueless what might happen when we fail to find an eight-card major fit.

Ideally we could access a magical software solution that would (1) deal thousands of suitable hands for opener and responder (2) test various algorithms to find the optimum scramble strategy (3) do the scrambles (4) play each deal in both 1NT and the scramble contract (5) compare the results and arrive at some conclusion. Alas that remedy does not exist, so we must be creative, and tackle the issue piecemeal.

To illustrate what data we expect to garner from our plan of attack, here is a very small sample of results pitting 1NT against 2♠ when there is a 4-4 fit. When completed, the full study will include thousands of deals for many different trump fits in many different scramble contracts.

2♠ vs 1NT With a 4-4 Spade Fit

(1) 2♠ Score	(2) 1NT Score	Diff (1)-(2)	2♠ IMPs Won	2♠ MPs Won
+170	+150	+20	+1	+1
+140	-50	+190	+5	+1
-100	-100	0	0	0
+110	+90	+20	+1	-1
-50	+90	-140	-4	+1
+140	+120	+20	+1	+1
+140	-100	+240	+6	+1
+110	-50	+160	+4	+1
+110	+120	-10	0	-1
+110	-100	+210	+5	+1

At IMPs, scrambles win +19

At Matchpoints, scrambles win 7, tie 1, lose 2

For these 10 deals, 2♠ outscored 1NT by an average of 1.9 IMPs. Although the sample size is tiny, it's beginning to point to a win for 2♠. When matchpointing, 2♠ beats 1NT seven times, ties once, and loses twice. How realistic do those numbers look to you? As you will see later, a more exhaustive analysis favours 2♠ even more convincingly.

Our initial task is to consider which kinds of hand should responder consider to scramble?

How Do We Do the Scrambles?

To help answer these questions, we enlist the help of a commercial double dummy solver (DDS). The DDS will deal 'suitably constrained' hands to opener and responder, and 'play' all deals in every strain. The DDS plays 'perfectly' both offence and defence. It finds all killing leads, every position knows whether the spot lead is from singleton or doubleton, and declarer drops all stiff offside kings. You've seen a DDS in action, they generate hand records for club and tournament results.

In addition, we need better 'reporting' than the solver offers. The DDS deals and plays out the deals, but it cannot step through the scramble motions to determine the scramble contract; it wasn't designed for that. So we simply designed and built an *extension, an augmentation* to the DDS. We won't bore you with the details, suffice to say the author programmed Bridge Buff, an early bridge-playing program.

With the augmented DDS, we do this:

- We shuffle deals with appropriate constraints for the opener and responder hands.
- We apply the scramble algorithm (in effect, 'bidding' the hands) to arrive at a scramble contract.
- We compare the double dummy score for the scramble contract with the score for 1NT.
- We measure the scoring difference in both IMPs, and a matchpoint metric.
- We repeat for thousands of hands.
- We like the result so much we share it in a book.

It is a valid application of DDS to compare results between 1NT and the scramble contract. We're not evaluating human playing computer, we're comparing DDS playing some suit contract with DDS playing the same cards in 1NT. That difference *is a reasonable proxy* for the difference in results for human play. DDS play will be stronger than most human play, but DDS suit-play is not relatively stronger than DDS notrump-play, or vice versa. The DDS and human scoring differences should be acceptably close for our purposes.

By the way, Richard Pavlicek on his great website, has convincing evidence (http://tinyurl.com/doubledummy) that top-flight human players do in fact play very nearly at DDS levels, even better! How could expert declarers play better than DDS? Well the human declarers are not faced with those killing double dummy leads. The DDS leader 'sees' all the cards. I hear that human opponents sometimes make unfortunate leads, so the human declarer benefits from that.

First we must decide what is an appropriate hand for opener to bid 1NT. We're focusing on weak notrumps, so we will begin by looking at opener with 12-14 HCP. Obviously we will include 4333 and 4432 hands, as well as 5332 holdings with a five-card minor. The modern trend is to include five-card majors in 1NT, so we will follow suit (although we investigate *not* including them later). We will also include (42)(52) shapes.

We don't know yet with certainty which hands are suitable for responder, that is one of our objectives, so we will take a look at a wide variety of them. Where should we start looking for *scramble-worthy* shapes? I'm not a good guesser, so how about we examine *all* responder shapes? As a baseline preview, we can apply the scramble *to each and every pattern*, barring obvious single-suiters and two-suiters.

Scramble Results for Various Specific Shapes

The following table summarizes comparisons of scramble contracts vs 1NT, for those various responder holdings. Throughout the tables, with interchanged minors, say 1-4-5-3 and 1-4-3-5, produce the same results (but see later for passing 2♦). The sample size for each is several thousand, so the margin of error is inconsequential.

For an IMP table (International Match Point), see Appendix II. For example, if the scramble contract is 2♥ making with an overtrick, scoring 140 compared to 90 for 1NT, that 50 point gain is worth 2 IMPs.

The matchpoint gains are a simple measure of which contract scores higher. The above-mentioned 2♥ contract would score one 'win'. Had 2♥ failed, it would score one 'loss'. About 10% of comparisons are 'ties', which reflect equal downtricks. A scoring difference of less than 20 (+110 compared to +120, say), is a matchpoint 'win' but an IMP 'gain' of zero. The incidence of ties is strongly correlated with responder's range. That is, there will be more (fewer) ties when responder is weaker (stronger).

For each of the following holdings, opener has a hand suitable to open a weak 1NT. Responder with a specific shape and 8-9 HCP scrambles to one of 2♥, 2♠, 3♣ or 3♦. These tables summarize the net aggregate score for those contracts compared to 1NT. 'Win' is the percentage of times the scramble contract scores higher than 1NT.

Specific Responder Shapes

Responder Shape	IMPs	--- Matchpoint % ---			Include?
		Win	Tie	Lose	
5-4-x-x	+2.1	76	7	17	Y
4-5-x-x	+2.5	82	5	13	Y
4-4-3-2	+0.9	59	13	28	Y
4-4-4-1	+1.9	71	8	21	Y
4-4-5-0	+2.6	79	4	17	Y
4-3-3-3	-1.4	30	14	56	N
4-3-4-2	+0.0	47	15	38	N
4-3-5-1	+1.3	63	10	27	Y
4-3-6-0	+1.8	66	7	27	Y
4-2-4-3	-0.7	41	13	46	N
4-2-5-2	+0.8	58	12	30	Y
4-2-6-1	+1.5	67	9	24	Y
4-1-4-4	+0.1	53	10	37	N
4-1-5-3	+0.7	58	10	32	Y
4-1-6-2	+1.5	67	9	24	Y
4-0-5-4	+0.8	61	9	30	Y
3-4-4-2	+0.1	49	14	37	N
3-4-5-1	+1.3	65	10	25	Y
3-4-6-0	+2.0	70	5	25	Y
3-2-4-4	-2.9	21	12	67	N
3-2-5-3	-1.5	29	13	58	N
3-2-6-2	-0.2	43	13	44	N
2-4-4-3	-1.7	35	11	54	N
2-4-5-2	+0.4	55	11	34	Y
2-4-6-1	+1.5	66	9	25	Y
2-3-4-4	-2.4	25	11	64	N
1-4-4-4	-1.3	41	7	52	N
1-4-5-3	+0.4	53	10	37	Y
1-4-6-2	+1.2	66	9	25	Y

* *Include* is Yes or No to whether the responder shape looks qualified to scramble.

A table entry reads like this. When responder holds 3-4-5-1 (for example) and exits 1NT for a scramble contract, he gains an average of +1.3 IMPs. That average is measured over thousands of deals and multiple scramble contracts. The scramble contract score beats the 1NT score 65% of the time, ties it 10%, and loses to it 25%. We 'include' this holding as a 'qualifying shape'.

So browsing the table, which responder distributions are clearly *not* suitable? 4333 is out, no surprise there. Except for 4-4-(32), the 4432 collection is problematic, some working not badly, some poorly. What common denominators are there? Obviously major-heavy holdings (54)xx and 4-4-xx should scramble, and equally obviously the flatter shapes should not, but are there a couple of generalities we can spot?

Ahhh there it is. If responder has both a four-card major and at least a five-card minor, he should scramble. It makes sense. The long minor serves as an 'escape valve' when you can't locate a major fit.

> *Hands which qualify to scramble include (1) (45)xx or 4-4-xx majors (2) hands with a four-card major and at least a five-card minor.*

Given that definition, responder is dealt a qualifying shape about 20% of the time. Some 40% of his holdings will be unbalanced one-suiters or two-suiters. About another 40% will be 4333 or 4432 not including both majors, or will not have a four-card major, and are best played in 1NT.

There is also a group of hands which benefit, but more weakly, the (43)(42) holdings. We will deal later with this group, which total about 7% of all responder hands.

Example: Deconstructing the 4-1-5-3 Holding

This shape generates fair but not great scramble contracts, with *fair* meaning you should still happily do the scramble. The previous table informs us the scramble contracts gain on average 0.7 IMPs compared to playing in 1NT. When the scramble scores are compared to 1NT scores, the scrambles score higher --- *matchpoint* better --- 58% of the time, tie 10%, and lose 32%. The scramble contract succeeds 70% of the time, 1NT 65%.

How do we know this? We randomly deal thousands of hands where opener has 12-14 HCP (balanced, including all 5332, and (42)(52)). Responder has 8-9 HCP with specifically 4-1-5-3 shape. We also gently constrain the opponent hands from being too weird. Slight variations from these constraints matter little.

For each suitable deal, opener and responder 'step through' the scramble routines to land in a contract. With 4-1-5-3 hands, sometimes we hit on a 5-4 spade fit (when opener has five spades), sometimes a 4-4 spade fit, sometimes a 4-3 spade fit, sometimes a 5-x diamond fit. For this exercise we *did not permit* responder to pass a 2♦ response (we went on to look for a spade Moysian), so by passing 2♦ with the right hands, your results at the table might be slightly more favourable.

Both 1NT and the scramble contract are put through a double dummy analysis. Scores are compared.

Let's *grade* the scramble outcomes like so:

- ❑ 45% of the time, the scramble lands in a 2♠ Moysian (4-3 fit), which matchpoints *slightly* better than 1NT. That is, 2♠ outscores 1NT narrowly (47% to 40%), say a 'B-' result.
- ❑ 24% of scramble contracts are 2♠ in a 4-4 fit. This contract plays hugely better than 1NT, scoring better than 1NT 89% of the time, and worse 7%. It's not remotely close. Call that an A+ outcome.
- ❑ 5% of the time opener will have five spades, and you'll play in your 5-4 spade fit which outscores 1NT 98% of the time. Call that an A++ outcome, although low frequency.
- ❑ The balance of the contracts (26%) are 3♦ (no spade fit).
  - ○ 3% are 5-2 fits. Opener was 2-4-2-5 and 3♦ scores poorly. Call that a very low frequency F outcome.
  - ○ 15% of the 3♦ contracts are 5-3 fits. They are modestly bad, not disasters. 3♦ matchpoints better 35% of the time, and worse 50%. Call that a D.
  - ○ 8% of the 3♦ contracts are 5-4 fits, which play very well. They outscore 1NT by a 3:1 ratio. Call that an A- outcome.

So the scramble outcomes for 4-1-5-3 hands, of B- (45%), A+ (24%), A++ (5%), F (3%), D (15%) and A- (8%), generate a pretty good net *decent* outcome. Grade the overall outcome for that shape at B, or so.

The fact that scrambles are net winners, matters little by vulnerability, by strength of 1NT opener, or by strength of responder. For example when 15-17 is opposite 3-4 with 4-

1-5-3, scrambles score better 57% and worse 23%, with an average IMP gain of about 1.3.

The Scramble Contract 'Landscape'

We've seen the scramble scores for specific shapes. Now, we want to see the outcome for the *ensemble of qualifying responder hands*, in the aggregate. This would proxy your net position over a long period of time. For example, in the first deal opener might be 3-4-4-2 opposite responder's 4-4-3-2, the next hand is 5-3-3-2 opposite 4-2-2-5, then 3-2-4-4 when responder is 5-4-2-2, and so on. We deal a very large sample of hands. Each deal is played in both a scramble contract, and 1NT. Opener has 12-14 HCP, responder 8-9. Where does the scramble take us, how often, and how do the scores compare?

The primary scramble contracts are 2♥ and 2♠ (generically call them 2M) and 3♣ and 3♦ (3m). Trump for various contracts might be configured 4-3 (43M and 43m) or 5-3 or 5-4 or 4-4 or 5-5 (there are rare 5-2 minor fits which we include in the 43m category, and 6-3 fits which we include in the 54m grouping).

So what does the 'landscape' of scramble contracts look like, when we put all the qualifying hands into one large, properly randomized 'pot' of deals, and scramble them? Ultimately just how are those scramble contracts distributed?

The Scramble Contract Landscape

Contract	Frequency	IMP Gain	Matchpoint % Win	Tie	Lose
43M	35%	-0.2	42	13	45
44M	32%	+2.7	85	6	9
53M	6%	+2.3	85	6	9
54+M	12%	+3.2	92	3	5
43m	3%	-3.5	13	11	76
44m	0%	-0.0	0	0	0
53m	7%	-0.2	40	12	48
54+m	5%	+1.4	70	11	19
Total	100%	+1.3	65	9	26

Scramble Contracts Make 76% of Time, 1NT 62%

Notes: The '54+' shapes include some 5-5 fits, and some 6-3 minor fits. There are no 4-4 minor fits because the qualifying hand is either 'major-heavy' (and the scramble contract will be 2M), or it will have a five-card minor. The '43m' category includes some 52m fits. There are zero six card trump fits, because the scramble cannot result in a minor fit poorer than 5-2, by our qualifying rules.

The scramble contract is successful 76% of the time, whereas 1NT makes 62% of the time. That's a huge deal! You make about 25% more contracts by scrambling.

A table entry reads like this. When you scramble you will land in a (say) 5-4 major fit 12% of the time. For those 2M contracts, on average your IMP gain compared to 1NT will be +3.2. At matchpoints, the 2M contracts will outscore 1NT 92% of the time, will tie 3%, and will lose 5%.

That scale of improvement applies right across the line. When responder holds 6-7 HCP instead of 8-9 HCP, the scramble contract scores better than 1NT 61% of the time, ties 19%, and loses 20%. The scramble contract makes 51% compared to 1NT making just 28%.

Or for strong notrumpers, with 15-17 HCP opposite 5-6 HCP, scrambles win 66%, tie 10%, and lose 24%. The scramble contract makes 74% compared to 1NT making just 58%.

The matchpoint (MP) metric is a direct comparison of the scramble contract vs 1NT, measured as *win, tie, lose*. The 'ties' are equal numbers of downtricks. A scoring difference of 10 is an IMP tie (90 vs 100, say), but a matchpoint win or loss.

There are very significant matchpoint advantages to playing in an 8+ card major fit. Conversely there are serious deficiencies to playing in the very small number of 3m contracts --- but half the time you land in a good major fit, only 3% in a poor minor fit. Scoring for the 43M Moysians compared to 1NT, is approximately neutral.

Landscape Summary

Net Scramble Results

Scramble		--- Matchpoint % ---		
Contract	%	Win	Tie	Lose
8+ Major Fit	50	87	5	8
4-3 Moysian	35	42	13	45
8+ Minor	12	52	11	37
Poor Minor	3	13	11	76
Total	100	65	9	26

Scramble Contract Makes 76% of time, 1NT 62%

Measured over all hands, when matchpoint scoring: *the scramble contract wins 65%, ties 9%, and loses 26%.*

To scramble or not to scramble? It surely looks like a winning strategy, but *how* winning? What would it mean to your score in a typical 26-board matchpoint outing? You scramble to 2♠ scoring 110, instead of sitting for 1NT making 90. The 2♠ contract matchpoints better, but on average by how much? If 90 scores three matchpoints on a twelve top, will 110 score seven? eight? Less? More? And what about 140 vs 90, or 110 vs –50, etc?

With some educated guesses, for weak notrumpers playing in a strong notrump field with a 12-top, we've estimated for a matchpoint session *the average real gain to be in the range of two matchpoints.* Strong notrumpers see comparable benefits. See Appendix I for gritty details.

The 4432 Hands

The 4432 pattern is the most common, about 22% of all responder holdings. We know that 4-4-xx is a prime candidate to scramble, and (32)-4-4 is not, but what about the balance, the collections (42)(43) and (43)(42)?

We can write one off quickly. The (42)(43) collection does not scramble well. The major doubleton causes too many scrambles to end in poor minor contracts.

However there is scramble hope for the (43)(42) hands: since opener will never (by our definition) be 2-2-(54), he will always have at least a three-card major, which might match up with responder. So what exactly is the overall position?

It turns out that *scrambling with (43)(42) is modestly beneficial*, especially at matchpoints, and more so with a weaker responder. (43)-4-2 performs slightly better than (43)-2-4, because responder can guess to pass 2♦ with the former, but that pickup is small, because 90% of the contracts end in major fits of some kind.

Since the modest gains are happening to a relatively large number of hands, you should consider including those shapes in your scramble routine.

For the following analyses, we've allowed responder to pass 2♦, so the net results will be slightly more scramble-favorable than you might see in other tables in this book.

Opener has 12-14, responder is (43)(42)

Resp HCP	IMP Gain	Matchpoint % Win	Tie	Lose	Scramb Win %	1NT Win %
10	0.3	52	6	42	80	83
9	0.3	50	11	39	68	70
8	0.3	47	17	35	54	52
7	0.3	44	24	33	39	36
6	0.7	44	26	30	25	18
5	0.9	46	26	28	15	7

Opener has 15-17, responder is (43)(42)

Resp HCP	IMP Gain	Matchpoint % Win	Tie	Lose	Scramb Win %	1NT Win %
7	0.2	54	7	39	78	82
6	0.2	51	14	36	65	66
5	0.2	45	21	34	49	48
4	0.3	41	26	33	33	27
3	0.7	45	25	31	21	13

An entry reads like this. Responder scrambles with 4 HCP opposite 15-17 HCP. On average he gains 0.3 IMPs, the scramble contract win/tie/lose compared to 1NT is 41/26/33, the scramble contracts make 33%, and 1NT 27%.

The (43)(42) hands end in 8+ major fits 35% of the time, in Moysians 55%, and in minor-suit fits 10%, only 3% bad.

1NT can make slightly more often than the scramble contract, but lose overall when matchpointing.

Or, the Hands You Should *Not* Scramble

It might be instructive to list the hands that should *not* qualify, instead of itemizing the acceptable ones.

Single Suiters: Generally speaking, if you have a five-card major or a majorless six-card minor, you should just transfer to them (but scramble with (54)xx hands).

Otherwise, *it is generally right to scramble if you have a four-card major, with about three exceptions.*

4333: These usually play poorly in a suit contract. Sure, if opener has say 4-2-5-2 opposite your 4-3-3-3, 2♠ will usually be a better contract, but leaving 1NT is a poor gamble.

(42)(43): Too often you will default to a bad minor fit. You need an *escape valve*, either a secondary major (even a three-carder), or a five-card minor. Compare with *(43)(42)* contracts, which scramble OK.

(41)(44): This is half OK, half not. 4-1-4-4 scrambles OK, 1-4-4-4 does not. The former catches spade Moysians, but the latter misses heart Moysians when opener has spades, and you will be playing to too many bad minor contracts, even if you pass 2♦. But if you can remember the distinction, include 4-1-4-4.

(32)xx: This one just doesn't work. There are not enough majors, and at the same time insufficient minors.

Example Auctions

Since the scramble begins 2♣, the bidding structure must also accommodate standard invitational Stayman sequences. Opener's initial replies are Stayman-like. *The key to the scramble is that either hand can check back for Moysians.* When you identify a 4-3 major fit, you consider your scramble a 'success' and 'settle' for it. Yes you end up playing many Moysians. Finally, failing to negotiate any kind of major fit, responder simply bids his longer minor. With rare exceptions the scramble ends with 2M and 3m contracts.

Either hand can abandon searching for a Moysian. If responder, he simply bids his longer minor like here: 1NT 2♣; 2♠ 3♦ (responder had four hearts, and not three spades, and five diamonds). If opener is doing the 'resigning', he bids 2NT (or 3♣) like here: 1NT 2♣; 2♦ 2♠; 2NT. Opener has neither a four-card major nor three spades, so bids 2NT to say to responder 'we tried but failed, bid your longer minor'. You could use 3♣ to ask the same question (responder passes or corrects) so you can distinguish between the two bids --- maybe 3♣ shows five clubs, or 2NT is a minimum and 3♣ a maximum.

For the most part the algorithm plays out automatically, in the sense neither party need apply any *judgement* --- with an exception or two coming up later. If the result stinks, blame the system. Except it rarely will.

Think of Scramble Stayman as basic 2♣ Stayman with Moysian checkbacks. Some examples follow.

	Opener		Responder
♠	A 7 6 5	♠	K 10 3
♥	K 10 7 6	♥	A J 9 8
♦	A Q 6	♦	10
♣	10 8	♣	9 7 5 4 2

1NT	12-14	2♣	Scramble
2♥	Have 4+	P	I ♥ this system

Opener has the hand responder was hoping for. Whatever the merits of 1NT, 2♥ will normally score better, with ruffs in either or both hands. The thing about even AKQJ opposite 10987 is this: played in 1NT, it can only ever ever take four tricks. In a spade contract, it cannot take fewer than four, and can in theory take up to eight.

The 4-4M fit is the workhorse of the scramble method. It arises a lot, accounting for nearly a third of the scramble contracts. The average IMP gain is a very significant 2.7, and *2M will matchpoint better than 1NT about 85% of the time.*

Let me repeat that. *2M will matchpoint better than 1NT about 85% of the time.*

	Opener		Responder
♠	A 7 6 5	♠	K 10 3
♥	K 10 7	♥	A J 9 8
♦	A Q 6	♦	10
♣	10 8 6	♣	9 7 5 4 2

1NT	12-14	2♣	Scramble
2♠	Have 4+	P	Settles in likely 4-3

Here responder has hopes for four hearts in opener, but 'settles' for the spade Moysian. Opener could also have five spades on this auction (about a 20% chance), in which case they 'recover' their 5-3 spade fit, which they initially 'lost' by choosing to include five-card majors in 1NT.

Moysians are the *reluctant suitor* contracts in the scramble routine. Modern bidding systems tend to avoid playing them. They can be technical and tricky, but not infrequently they play quite well. Ironically, often a scrambly-type of play is the winning strategy. If one has the right attitude, they're challenging and fun. And when 2M makes, it usually outscores 1NT. The question is, over a large sample, how often do Moysians win, and how do they score?

	Opener		Responder
♠	A 7 6 5	♠	K 10 3 2
♥	K 10 7 6	♥	A J 9
♦	A Q 6	♦	10
♣	10 8	♣	9 7 5 4 2

1NT	12-14	2♣	Scramble
2♥	Have 4+	P	Settles for likely 4-3 fit

Scramble Stayman does not always locate the theoretical optimal fit, although it is a huge favourite to do so, in the 95% range. Here responder settles for a 4-3 heart fit, and misses the far lovelier 4-4 spades. These imperfections are unavoidable, but are relatively infrequent with minimal impact on the overall results. Note they find their 5-3 heart fit when opener is 3-5-3-2.

Responder cannot risk a 2♠ call, hoping opener has four spades, although opener happens to have four on this deal. With three spades, opener will pass 2♠, so you are trading Moysians. With two spades opener will bid 2NT, asking responder to bid his longer minor, and responder wouldn't like that option on this hand --- he'd rather be in his 2♥ Moysian than risk landing in a poor 3m contract. Also there is about a 20% chance opener will have five hearts making for a comfortable 5-3 fit.

However this example *is* a position where a relatively strong responder holding, say, KQxx AJT x xxxxx, *might* choose to risk a 2♠ bid. If opener has four spades they're in a much better spot. If opener has three spades he has traded Moysians, no problems. If opener holds just two spades he will bid 2NT to ask responder to bid his longer minor. With this hand responder will bypass his minors and rebid 3♥. Responder judges his hand an acceptable dummy even with just three trumps, and the gambit is worth the risk because he might find a four-four spade fit. It's also possible opener with two spades, will rebid 3♣ with some 2-4-2-5 hand and you land in a dandy 5-5 club fit (when opener declines major interest, 3♣ shows five clubs along the way to some 3m, otherwise he bids 2NT).

	Opener		Responder
♠	A 7 6	♠	K 10 3 2
♥	K 10 7 6	♥	A J
♦	A Q	♦	10 9 8 7 6
♣	10 8 6 4	♣	9 7

1NT	12-14	2♣	Scramble
2♥	Have 4+	2♠	Have 3 spades?
P	Yes I do		

Here responder hopes for four spades, but strikes out. After 2♥, responder checks back for the spade Moysian, and opener sits for 2♠.

What do you think are the chances of making 2♠? 1NT? Which would you rather be in? 2♠ looks very playable.

	Opener			Responder
♠	A 7 6 5		♠	K 10
♥	Q 10		♥	A J 9 8
♦	A Q 6		♦	10 9
♣	J 8 7 4		♣	10 9 7 5 2

1NT	12-14		2♣	Scramble
2♠	Have 4+		3♣	Bids longer minor

Having no major fit, responder bids his longer minor. This can sometimes lead to dicey contracts, but 3♣ here has great play, on a *very* good day making five (off two clubs with 2-2 split, with red kings onside).

The fewer major suit cards opener has, the more minors he will hold, so often responder's stab at 3m will land in a good spot. But sometimes not. Only 15% or so scramble contracts are 3♣ or 3♦, and only 3% poor.

	Opener		Responder
♠	A 7 6	♠	K 10 3 2
♥	K 10	♥	A J 9 8
♦	A Q 6 5 4	♦	10 9
♣	10 8 6	♣	9 7 5

1NT	12-14	2♣	Scramble
2♦	No 4-card M	2♥	Have 3 hearts?
2♠	No, but have 3 spades	P	Settles

Here is a typical scramble to the Moysian. Played in 1NT, the defence might grab four or five clubs and a couple of diamonds. Played in 2♠, the trumps will 'block' the run of the club suit, and 2♠ will have decent play.

Note when responder has both four hearts and four spades, he will always locate some kind of major fit (we assume 1NT with 22(45) not permitted).

	Opener		Responder
♠	A 7	♠	K 10 3 2
♥	K 10 5	♥	A J 9
♦	A Q 6 5	♦	10 9 8 7 2
♣	10 8 6 4	♣	9

1NT	12-14	2♣	Scramble
2♦	No 4-card M	P	

It's matchpoints and responder was hoping to hear 2♠, and would have been content to hear 2♥. However with that diamond holding, he's happy to pass 2♦. With a better diamond suit, one that he wouldn't mind playing in 3♦ if he must, he might judge to try first for the 2♠ Moysian.

	Opener		Responder
♠	A 7	♠	Q 10 9 8
♥	K 10 5	♥	A 4 2
♦	A Q 6	♦	K 10 9 8 7 5
♣	10 8 6 4 2	♣	5

1NT	12-14	2♣	Scramble
2♦	No 4-card M	2♠	Have 3 spades?
3♣	No, but I have 5 clubs	3♦	Hugely prefer diamonds

Responder thinks his hand will play nicely in a spade Moysian if it exists, and decides he won't mind playing in 3♦ as a fallback.

Here, opener helps responder judge the best minor position by showing his five clubs. Were responder 4-2-5-2, he would move out of 3♣ (the known 5-2 fit) to 3♦ (cannot be worse than 5-2).

Frequently the 3m contract makes, but when that's happening, often 1NT with overtricks scores better. Here, 1NT will usually score at least 150 (but who will be in game?), and 3♦ is big favorite to make a couple of overtricks for the same score. Scoring for a 3m contract on a 5-3 fit versus 1NT, is usually approximately neutral.

	Opener		Responder
♠	A 7 6 5	♠	3 2
♥	K 10 9	♥	A J 8 7
♦	A Q 6 5	♦	10 9
♣	10 8	♣	K J 9 7 4

Opener		Responder	
1NT	12-14	2♣	Scramble
2♠	Have 4+	3♣	Bids longer minor, must have hearts
3♥	Prefers play in 4-3 hearts to 5-2 clubs	P	You're the boss of me

This is an interesting position for opener, which he might have to 'think' about. Usually opener cedes captaincy to responder but occasionally he gets a full picture of responder's hand and takes charge of the auction.

Here, responder promises four hearts (by partnership agreement this scramble guarantees a four-card major, and responder denied three or four spades when he rebid 3♣). Opener judges his hand will play better in the (promised) 4-3 heart fit than a potential 5-2 fit, so he corrects to 3♥. Responder could also have six clubs with something like 1-4-2-6, in which case opener would have been better off passing.

The Minor-Suit Fallbacks

The minor-suit fits are played when you cannot locate a major-suit fit. They total some 15% of scramble contracts. When the search for a major fails, responder simply bids his longer minor. Obviously there is some luck involved. If opener is the one 'giving up' on finding a major fit, he usually asks responder with 2NT to bid his longer minor (but holding five clubs, opener could 'ask' with 3♣, if that is your agreement). Or perhaps your agreement is opener's 3♣ shows a minimum, and 2NT a maximum.

Here, responder bows out and bids 3♦: 1NT 2♣; 2♠ 3♦. Responder had four hearts and five diamonds, opener four spades.

Here, opener surrenders with 2NT: 1NT 2♣; 2♥ 2♠; 2NT. Opener had four hearts and not three spades. Responder had four spades and not three hearts.

Here, opener gives up and shows five clubs in the process: 1NT 2♣; 2♥ 2♠; 3♣. Opener was 2-4-2-5.

Overall you will land in a major-suit contract about 85% of the time --- 35% Moysian, 32% in a 4-4 fit, 6% in a 5-3 fit, 12% in a 5-4 or 5-5 fit. So responder falls back to some minor fit about 15% of the time.

Of the 15% minor-suit contracts, some 5% are 5-4 and 5-5 fits, which you want to be in. They outscore 1NT. About 7% are 5-3 fits, which score about as well as 1NT. The remaining 3% are poorly performing 5-2 and 4-3 contracts.

It is important to remember these bad results are rare. Good scramble contracts overwhelm them. You'll find

SEVENTEEN times the 8+ major fits for every seven-card minor fit. That looks like an excellent trade-off.

The Moysians

Overall, the Moysians perform about as well as 1NT, but context plays a role of course. Any shortness in either hand, especially the three-trump hand, can be a measurable help. Responder with 4-3-1-5 is happy to find himself in a 2♥ Moysian (diamond ruffs in short hand!)

Say there is no shortness. Give opener 12-14 with 3xxx, and responder 8-9 with *balanced* 4xxx. 2♠ makes 45% of the time, but 1NT makes 63%. 2♠ also loses at matchpoints with win/tie/lose percentages = 31/16/53

However give opener the same hands with 3xxx, but responder some unbalanced 4(135). Now 2♠ makes 65%, 1NT 63%, but 2♠ matchpoints stronger with win/tie/lose = 53/12/35. That shortness makes a huge difference, even in the long-trump hand.

For the ensemble of responder hands making up the 'landscape', in total Moysians are about as neutral with 1NT as you can get, with some deals playing a little better than 1NT, some a little worse.

Scramble Factoids

The scramble gains are remarkably consistent across all opening ranges for 1NT, most HCP ranges for responder, and any vulnerability. In addition, it makes little difference whether or not opener can have a five-card major, or if opener can have some (42)(52).

Actually as responder gets weaker, the scramble gains *increase*. Making 1NT with 12 opposite 6 or 15 opposite 3, is unlikely, but those major-suit fits might scramble home, and at least have a chance of not failing by so many tricks.

Variations on a Theme

	IMP Gain	--- Matchpoint % ---		
		Win	Tie	Lose
(1) 12-14 opp 8-9 Can have 5M	1.30	65	9	26
12-14 opp 8-9 As (1), NonVul	1.16	65	9	26
12-14 opp 8-9 As (1), no 5M	1.15	63	10	27
12-14 opp 8-9 As (1), no (42)(52)	1.18	65	9	26
12-14 opp 6-7 Can have 5M	1.86	62	17	21
12-14 opp 4-5 Can have 5M	2.61	64	19	17
15-17 opp 5-6 Can have 5M	1.36	66	10	24
15-17 opp 5-6 Cannot have 5M	1.22	64	10	26
10-12 opp 10-11 Can have 5M	1.40	66	9	25

For Strong Notrumpers

We've focused on 12-14 openers because the scramble position arises much more often than it does for 15-17 openers. However strong notrumpers also benefit considerably. Opponent interference is also less likely to disrupt the scramble. We see the same approximate results when 15-17 is opposite 5-6 --- scrambling creates a gain of about one IMP per scramble, and matchpoint results follow the same pattern, about 65% score better than 1NT, 10% tie, and 25% score worse.

Notice ties increasing as responder's hand declines in value --- there are increasingly more equal downtricks.

Holdings	IMP Gain	--- Matchpoint% ---		
		Win	Tie	Lose
15-17 opposite 7	1.07	68	4	28
opposite 6	1.21	67	8	25
opposite 5	1.56	65	12	23
opposite 4	1.96	65	17	18
opposite 3	2.32	63	19	18

For weak notrumpers in a strong notrump field, the benefit from scrambling is partly due to 'catching up to' the matchpoint field, who have already found their major-suit fits.

For strong notrumpers in a strong notrump field, the scrambling benefit is due to simply landing in better contracts more often. Say the entire field is bidding 1NT and scoring up +90. You score an average 6 on a 12 top. If 65% of the time you can scramble to a higher-scoring contract, 10% tie, and 25% lose to 1NT, what happens?

What happens is 65% of the time you will score a top (12 matchpoints), 10% will score an average (6), and 25% score a bottom (0). That computes, over time, to an average scramble matchpoint score of 8.4, compared to your conservative stay-in-1NT 6.

Free matchpoints!

Efficiency at Finding Fits

You do the scramble because it finds you major-suit fits that you would miss if you pass 1NT. How efficient is it? The routine cannot locate *100%* of existing fits for reasons discussed previously, but just what fraction of theoretical fits does it find for you?

(For example, here the scramble misses a 4-4 spade fit. Opener is 4-4-3-2 and responds 2♥. Responder is 4-3-5-1 and passes 2♥, settling for the heart Moysian.)

Using the original definition of 'qualifying' hands ((54)xx, 4-4-xx, four-card major with five-card minor), about 50% of scramble contracts are 8+ major-suit fits. It turns out the scrambles find 95% of the 5-4 fits, 93% of the 4-4 fits, and about half of the (lower-frequency) 5-3 fits.

In total, the scrambles find about 85% of the existing 8+ major-suit fits.

On average those fits all play better than 1NT, some considerably so, and unless you embark on a scramble, *you don't find them.*

However it is important to remember, even when you miss a 4-4 fit to settle in a Moysian, that 4-3 contract over time will score about as well as 1NT. So the upside is very good, the downside very minimal.

What Percentage of Hands Qualify?

If you limit your scrambles to those delicious (54)xx hands, you include only 4.4% of all responder hands (within HCP range). Let's add some pieces. Remember our qualifying rule: *(1) major-heavy hands plus (2) hands with a four-card major plus a five- or six-card minor.*

- ❏ Start with (54)xx hands, at 4.4% of all holdings

- ❏ 4-4-xx hands add 5.4%
- ❏ (42)(52) hands add 3.5%
- ❏ (43)(51) hands add 2.2%
- ❏ (41)(53) hands add 2.2%
- ❏ (42)(61) hands add 0.8%
- ❏ (41)(62) hands add 0.8%
- ❏ (40)(54) hands add 0.4%
- ❏ (40)(63) hands add 0.2%
- ❏ (43)(60) hands add 0.2%

In total those pieces add to 20.1%, which is double the qualifiers of a "Crawling Stayman" agreement which applies to (44)xx and (54)xx hands. (Also you will be scrambling over a far wider responder HCP range than the typical Crawling Stayman arrangement.)

Very roughly, responder's hands (within range) will consist of 20% scramblers, 40% one- and two-suiters, and 40% which are primarily balanced but don't qualify to scramble, consisting largely of the 4333 and 4432 shapes (excluding the 4-4-xx hands of course).

If you include the weaker (43)(42) qualifiers, you increase the number of qualifying hands to about 27% of all responder holdings.

Meshing With "Standard" Stayman

You easily overlay most of 'standard' Stayman, with the following provisos:

1. If bidding 2♣ as normal invitational Stayman, you must have at least one four-card major.
2. With a no-major invitational hand and wanting to invite, use your system size-ask, typically 2♠ or 2NT. Playing four-suit transfers, 2♠ is often played as 'clubs or size ask', with opener rebidding 2NT to show a minimum, and 3♣ a maximum.
3. Locating an invitation in opener's major, raise the major with 3M, do not bid a secondary suit (which bid is often part of scramble routines).
4. With an invitation in the other major, responder rebids 2NT.

Some sequences to consider:

[1NT 2♣; 2♦ 2M] is a scramble bid in search of a Moysian, and will be passed by opener with three.

[1NT 2♣; 2♦ 3m] cannot be a scramble; after 2♦ scrambler will *always* hunt for Moysians with 2M.

[1NT 2♣; 2♥ 2♠] is a scramble.

[1NT 2♣; 2♥ 3m] cannot be a scramble; scrambler with hearts passes, or tries for a Moysian with 2♠.

[1NT 2♣; 2♠ 3m] shows responder scrambling with four hearts and fewer than three spades. With the right hand, opener hearing 3♣ *might* revert to 3♥ with say 4-3-4-2, hoping 4-3 hearts will outscore 5-2 clubs (odds generally favor the 5-2 to make more often, but when the Moysian succeeds, it scores very well).

[1NT 2♣; 2x 2NT] is a Stayman invitation with an unbid four-card major.

As a general rule, *scrambler* responder (1) after opener's 2♦ will always check back for a Moysian UNLESS he passes, thinking 2♦ will be a nice contract (2) after opener's 2♥ will always pass or rebid 2♠ (3) after opener's 2♠ will always pass or rebid 3m.

As a general rule, invitational-only *Stayman* responder (1) after opener's 2♦ will always rebid 2NT (2) after opener's 2♥ will always raise to 3♥ or rebid 2NT (3) after opener's 2♠ will always raise to 3♠ or rebid 2NT. This assumes you also employ a game-forcing Stayman bid, typically 3♣. If not, responder's choices here include various leaps to game.

Responder requires a four-card major to use Stayman because he cannot rebid 2M, that being a scramble checkback, so must rebid 2NT to show an unbid major. Lacking a major he initially invites with the system size-ask, and if your system doesn't have one, it should. Playing four-suit transfers, 2♠ stands in nicely for both clubs and size-ask (opener replies 2NT = minimum, 3♣ = maximum).

Stayman responder invites in opener's major only with a raise to 3M.

Stayman responder cannot use the 2M rebid to show some kind of invitational hand. If he does rebid 2M, he's scrambling.

The Price You Pay

The sequences 1NT 2♣; 2M 3m are allocated to scramble routines. They no longer can be used in your standard Stayman sequences.

You might previously have used 1NT 2♣; 2♥ 3♦ to show an invitational hand with four spades and five diamonds. Or you might have used that auction to go 'slamming', or shape-showing and game-forcing. You'll have to find another way to bid those holdings.

Maybe you simply not have an 'invitational' status for 4M5m hands, responder determining from the outset if they are game-worthy or not.

Perhaps slammish hands could start with an 'impossible' auction 1NT 2♣; 2♥ 3♠, or 1NT 2♣; 2♠ 3♥.

With a game-forcing hand you can start with the minor transfer, or with a game forcing 3♣ Stayman query.

There are other methods to handle those holdings, which we won't get into here.

Game Forcing Stayman with 3♣, and Smolen, mesh well with Scramble Stayman.

Miscellany

Pros Overwhelm Cons

Yes you will land in a teeny number of poor 3m fits that will score poorly. Just remember for every seven-card minor fit, you will land in SEVENTEEN 8+ major fits, the vast bulk of which will score considerably better than 1NT.

And yes you must learn how to master Moysian fits. They're fun to play (once you know the techniques), and score more or less the same as 1NT. The contract landscape suggests a Moysian will beat 1NT 42%, tie it 13%, and lose to it 45%. It's a basic coin-flip --- and your willingness to maybe play in one opens the door to negotiate all kinds of nice major-suit contracts. For what it's worth, here is an independent double-dummy assessment of Moysian vs 1NT in high-level play, which comes to the same coin-flip conclusion: *http://tinyurl.com/moysian.*

After Interference by 4th Hand

The 2♣ bidder will be considerably more likely to have a scrambling hand than an invitational Stayman hand … for weak notrumpers a range of say 0 to 10 HCP, compared to 11-12 HCP (assuming you use 3C as GF Stayman).

In my experience with weak notrumps, balancing seat will strain to find something to bid when faced with this:

(1NT)　P　(P)　??

He will strain less here.

(1NT)　P　(2♣)　??

Balancer will be more hesitant to act in part because his defensive methods might be disrupted with 2♣. Also it is dangerous to intervene with borderline values because responder with a good hand might be trotting out Stayman. At the point of the 2♣ bid, nobody but responder knows what kind of hand he has. For what it is worth, limited personal field experience illustrates that balancer *is much less likely to intervene over 2♣*. Much less.

If advancer does intervene, what should opener do? We know responder will have a four-card major. Depending on your agreed HCP range for a scramble attempt, he might be very weak, but he will have that four-card major. Given that, maybe it makes sense for opener to show possession of *both majors* with an immediate bid, so he doubles the 4th suit bid, or redoubles a double, or perhaps your arrangement is he bids 2♥ which is 'pass or correct'.

1NT	(P)	2♣	(2♦)
X =	both majors		

1NT	(P)	2♣	(X)
XX=	both majors		

If opener passes, when the bidding comes around to responder, he should double if his 2♣ was invitational Stayman, otherwise he should probably just pass unless he has a five-card major or six-card minor.

1NT	(P)	2♣	(2♦)
P	(P)	X = Stayman	

If responder sees a 'double' float around to him, he should redouble with Stayman, otherwise scramble.

```
1NT    (P)    2♣    (X)
 P     (P)    XX = Stayman
```

```
1NT    (P)    2♣    (X)
 P     (P)    2♥ = bail
```

Intervener's strategy might be to play 'notrump systems on' over 2♣, with double meaning whatever a 2♣ bid shows. Since responder can be quite good, intervener should have good values, or extra shape. If unclear what to do, he can always pass and come in later. Alternatively, a double of 2♣ might just show a good hand, protection against those situations when responder is weak.

HCP Range for Scramble Responder

How weak can (should) responder be, to scramble? He's less than invitational, but how low is the floor? Faced with impending doom, when responder just *knows* LHO is strong (partner has 12-14, RHO has a fast pass, and responder is looking at a lonely king, say), if his hand qualifies should he immediately scramble, or pass and hope that a good thing might happen? The good thing might be (1) intervener lacks a biddable suit, and is nervous making a general penalty double because 2♣ *might* be strong, and heck he will always have another crack at it when the auction returns to him (2) intervener might bid some suit, often taking responder off the hook (unless dastardly opener doubles to show both majors), (3) intervener might double but your RHO might 'rescue' him.

So with a qualifying shape, responder never passes! With less than invitational, he starts 2♣ Scramble. With invitational he starts 2♣ regular Stayman. With game-forcing, he starts whatever you are using for that, either 2♣ or 3♣.

Alternatively if responder chooses to pass and intervener doubles and it comes back to him, responder can always trot out his partnership's escape routine, whatever that is.

This system needs more field-testing, but my instincts go with playing the range to be 0 to 10 (0 to 7 for strong notrumpers), and immediately scrambling with all suitable hands, especially the major-heavy ones. Intervener might be more hesitant to act initially, and when it comes back around to him he won't have his impressive notrump defence to help him out.

Actually if the opponents are on their toes, they should use double of a (2C) response to show a generic good hand, just in case responder is running.

Sounds to me, as overcaller, that two-level doubles like (1NT) P (2♣) P; (2x) P (P) X or (1NT) P (2♣) P; (2x) P (2y) X, are best played as takeout.

Passing 2♦

When responder has long diamonds and opener denies a four-card major, responder gets the chance to pass 2♦, and should usually take it. Say responder holds Kxxx xx KTxxx xx and the auction proceeds 1NT 2♣; 2♦. Instead of checking back for a spade Moysian, not finding one and having to rebid 3♦, responder should choose to play in 2♦.

However at matchpoints where making 2♠ on a 4-3 fit looks like a good option, and you don't mind having to play in 3♦, you might consider checking back for the Moysian. Maybe you hold KQxx x QJ10xxx xx or the like. Your 2♠ try might also shut out a 2♥ balance.

Note all scrambling algorithms used in this book assume responder *will always check back for that Moysian.* We wanted to keep the algorithm free of judgement. To that extent, since you will from time to time pass 2♦, *your real-life results will slightly outperform our analysis.*

The 4333 Hands

In suit contracts, these hands usually play poorly, since they offer close to zero ruffing opportunities. When opener has four spades, and responder is 4-3-3-3, the contract usually belongs in notrump. Still, the notrump contract isn't *always* the winning spot, since *opener's hand* might provide ruffs. Opener with 4-2-5-2 opposite 4-3-3-3 will often play better in a spade contract, for example.

However in notrump contracts the 4333 pattern plays approximately as well as any other balanced hand. Consequently it doesn't make a lot of sense for opener to 'downgrade' his holding while deciding what to open. He can't read the future, he doesn't know in which strain the hand is going to be played. Some expert players, playing a strong notrump, will downgrade a 15 HCP 4333 holding to be 'worth' just 14 points, and not open 1NT. That doesn't seem right to us.

Here are some observations. Opener has a balanced hand with four spades and 15-17 HCP. When responder is precisely 4-3-3-3 and has 8-9 HCP, 4S makes 30% and 3NT makes 32%, a virtual tie. However give responder a doubleton, say 4-3-4-2, and 4S makes 44% while 3NT makes 36%. The spade contract also matchpoints much better than the notrump contract.

Extending Scramble to 1NT *Rebids*

The scramble principle can be extended to 1NT *rebids*. Weak notrumpers will normally rebid 1NT with a range of about 15-17, and strong notrumpers will have 11/12 to 14 or so. *Responder would scramble only when holding four cards in the unbid major.*

Raising *styles* influence the way the scramble plays out. Say as opener you hold a 13 HCP 4-3-2-4 hand, and open 1♣. Partner responds 1♥. Some pairs would raise to 2♥ (and responder with a strong hand would later sort out the type of raise), some would rebid 1NT, and some might even rebid 1♠ (that would be more likely with 4-2-3-4).

This scramble algorithm assumes opener will *not* raise with only three trumps.

When scrambling and responder initially responds 1♥, he will be 4-4-xx or 4-5-xx. Compared to passing the 1NT rebid, he will gain about one IMP per hand, and he will matchpoint 60% better, 30% worse, with 10% ties.

When he responds 1♠, responder will be 5-4-xx. That holding gains about 0.5 IMPs, and matchpoints 55% better, 10% ties and 35% worse.

Solves Awkward 'Conditionally-Invitational' Hands

These are those hands which increase in value from partial-strength to invitational, *if you have a major fit*. They are *conditionally invitation-worthy*. As responder you pick up KQxx x AT9xx xxx. When opener is 12-14, that's a tough hand to bid. Despite having only 9 HCP, if opener has spade help and a good hand, 4♠ will have a shot. Or for strong notrumpers, think Kxxx x AT9xx xxx. If opener has a four spades, you'd happily invite in his suit. But if he doesn't, you'll have to rebid 2NT, and partner will too often raise that problematic contract to a surely unmakeable game. Using Scramble Stayman, you don't mind scrambling for a spade fit, with 3♦ as fallback. If partner shows four spades, you will invite with a 3♠ bid.

Other 1NT positions

You might consider to employ Scramble Stayman in almost any position where you use standard Stayman, for example when you *overcall/reopen* with 1NT:

	(1x)	1NT	(P)	2♣

	(1x)	P	(P)	1NT
	(P)	2♣		

	1x	(1y)	P	(P)
	1NT	(P)	2♣	

Vulnerability a Small Factor

Most of the preceding analysis has been based on both sides being vulnerable, with downtricks being –100 apiece. However –200 is a killer at matchpoints. Some of the poorer contracts result scramble scores of –200 or worse, more often than 1NT ... the occasional but rare extra bottom. It might be prudent for borderline cases when vulnerable, to not scramble (the (43)(42) hands for example). The 'challenge match' is both sides non-vulnerable (mixed, or only vulnerable, would make virtually no difference).

No Five-Card Major in Opener not a Factor

Well, maybe just a surprisingly small factor, and you should adapt Scramble Stayman anyway. When your opener does include 5M332 hands, you obviously locate more 5-4 fits and 5-3 fits than you would otherwise.

With 5-card majors, the line for scrambling is +1.30 IMPs, Win/Tie/Lose at matchpoints is 65/9/26. *Without* 5-card majors the line is +1.15 IMPs, 63/10/27 for matchpoints.

Scrambles Occur a *LOT*

They do for weak notrumpers anyway. Opener is dealt 12-14 about twice as often as 15-17. Responder is dealt 0 to 10 (qualifying range opposite a weak notrump) about twice as often as 0 to 7. Together that means scramble opportunities will arise *several times as often* for weak notrumpers. Almost makes it worthwhile to switch, eh?

Strong notrumps are less likely to be overcalled however, so the occasion for them isn't *disrupted* as often.

"Recover" Many Five-card Majors

The modern trend is to open 1NT with 5M332 hands. The justification for strong notrumpers is when they open 1M with 15-17, it makes for a difficult rebid.

The justification for weak notrumpers is not as convincing, especially if the five-suit is spades. Opening 1NT with a five-card heart suit makes sense, because it prevents an easy 1♠ overcall, or takeout double of a 1♥ opening. Also if weak notrumpers play 'balanced club' (1♣ is either standard unbalanced, or 15-19 balanced), including 5M332 in 1NT is a good idea because now your 1♦/♥/♠ openers are unbalanced.

Anyway you will often lose 5-3 and 5-4 major partials when you open 1NT. Scrambling will recover many of those fits.

Scramble Stayman (SS) vs Crawling Stayman (CS)

CS is kind of a *subset* of SS. SS will arise far more often than CS, due to two major differences.

SS is played over a much wider range of responder *distributions*, either 20% of hands (using the 'stronger' qualifiers only) or closer to 30% (when including the 'weaker' qualifiers). CS is sometimes played with just (54)xx hands at 4%, but often includes 4-4-xx hands to total 10%.

In addition, SS is played over a much wider range of responder *strength*. We suggest 0 to just-less-than-invitational. CS is usually limited to weak hands.

Whether you play Crawling Stayman at all (surely you will now want some of those free masterpoints), or play a limited or extended version of it, you have been guessing at its 'value'. If nothing else, this book has validated its use.

Implications for Other Bidding Areas

Consider the very common sequence 1m 1M; 2M. Some pairs play that in order to raise responder's 1M bid, opener *must* have 4 trumps. However we have considerable 'proof' that 4-3 Moysians play as well as 1NT, so immediately raising with three trumps (provided opener is not 4333), has considerable merit.

Say opener with Ax Kxx KQxx Jxxx is playing a strong notrump system. He opens 1♣ and partner responds 1♥. Many pairs would rebid 1NT in that position. However we've seen that 2♥ will score well, and has the added benefit of being more pre-emptive. If responder happens to have invitational or better strength, he can now sort out the details of opener's raise, maybe starting with a 2NT query.

Conclusions

- ❏ You're playing way too many 1NT contracts.
- ❏ Consider this. When responder has a partial-strength 4-4 spade fit, 2♠ will matchpoint better than 1NT by nearly a nine to one ratio.
- ❏ And this. The average scramble contract will make 76% of the time, compared to 62% for 1NT. Make 25% more of your contracts.
- ❏ And this. Of all possible responder hands within HCP range, some 20% will meet the requirements to scramble to a better spot. Make that 27% if you scramble with the 'weaker' (43)(42) qualifiers, which are quite effective especially when responder has a poor hand. Exit 1NT *before* they start doubling.
- ❏ When you do scramble, you will land in an 8+ major fit 50% of the time.
- ❏ Results are consistent for any opening range (mini, weak, strong), any vulnerability, whether or not 1NT includes 5M332 and/or (42)(52), and for any responding range.
- ❏ Consider the 1NT opener not only as a place to play, but for some holdings as a launchpad to better partials.
- ❏ You will improve your score by an average of about two matchpoints in a twelve-top session. Weak notrumpers will return to field results, and strong notrumpers will play better contracts than the field.
- ❏ You now have a solution to those *conditionally invitation-worthy* hands. You will have methods to deal with Kxxx xx Axxxx Kx, and the like, when partner opens a weak notrump.
- ❏ And don't forget that 1NT (P) 2♣ makes it a lot tougher for 4th seat to bid, than 1NT (P) P.

100 Deal Challenge Match

We will play a 100 board 'challenge match'. Sitting South at one 'table' will be Scramble Stayman guy. Sitting at another will be 1NT dude, who passes every hand. Both are dealt the same hands. The deals are constrained by our requirements that opener have a 12-14 balanced hand suitable to open 1NT (included are 5M332 and (42)(52)), and responder have the kind of hand we have negotiated --- 8-9 HCP, a four-card major, no long biddable suit, not 4333, etc. Within that context, the hands are random, generating the 'right' numbers of the various distributions (excluded are the 'weaker qualifiers' (43)(42)).

We also (very crudely) constrained the opponent's hands to ones they would likely pass. Both opponents were unlikely to hold good hands with long suits for example, or high HCP hands. However there will be some defender hands that you (or we) would bid. Just ignore that circumstance, and concentrate on the opener/declarer pair of hands.

We used a commercial program to compose these deals with the familiar constraints. For each deal we ran double dummy results exactly like you see on hand records at your club and tournaments. We mentally stepped through the scramble algorithm to arrive at a scramble contract. We then compared scores for that contract with scores for 1NT, and kept a running tally.

We were interested to see how close this small-sample experiment would agree (within sampling error) with the larger analysis. To simplify comparisons, everybody is non-vulnerable, opener plays all contracts, and we applied 'zero' judgement so responder never passes 2♦. The match is on!

Deal # 1

	♠	KT4
	♥	KJ
	♦	QJ942
	♣	A65

1N 2♣; then
2♦ 2♥; 2♠

♠	J63		♠	A87
♥	QT963		♥	A4
♦	T8		♦	K753
♣	Q94		♣	J872

	♠	Q952
	♥	8752
	♦	A6
	♣	KT3

	2♠	1N
type	43M	
scor	+170	+120
IMP	+2	
MP	+1	

Tot IMP   +2

---- Tot MP ---

Win	Tie	Loss
1	0	0

Deal # 2

	♠	A87
	♥	9532
	♦	AT83
	♣	A4

1N 2♣; then
2♥

♠	T62		♠	J95
♥	KJ		♥	AT7
♦	K74		♦	J965
♣	KJ732		♣	Q95

	♠	KQ43
	♥	Q864
	♦	Q2
	♣	T86

	2♥	1N
type	44M	
scor	+140	-50
IMP	+5	
MP	+1	

Tot IMP   +6

---- Tot MP ---

Win	Tie	Loss
2	0	0

	♠	AQ2
	♥	A8
	♦	Q8632
	♣	Q84

Deal # **3**

1N 2♣; then

2♦ 2♥; 2♠

	2♠	1N

♠	JT3	♠	974
♥	K62	♥	Q74
♦	AJT95	♦	K4
♣	72	♣	AT965

type	43M	
scor	+110	+90
IMP	+1	
MP	+1	

	♠	K865
	♥	JT953
	♦	7
	♣	KJ3

Tot IMP   +7

---- Tot MP ---

Win	Tie	Loss
3	0	0

	♠	QT5
	♥	92
	♦	AK87
	♣	A763

Deal # **4**

1N 2♣; then

2♦ 2♥; 2♠

	2♠	1N

♠	KJ76	♠	4
♥	J64	♥	AK73
♦	T4	♦	QJ9532
♣	QJ85	♣	94

type	53M	
scor	+140	+90
IMP	+2	
MP	+1	

	♠	A9832
	♥	QT85
	♦	6
	♣	KT2

Tot IMP   +9

---- Tot MP ---

Win	Tie	Loss
4	0	0

Deal # 5

	♠	53
	♥	KJ62
	♦	AJ6
	♣	KT52

1N 2♣; then
2♥

♠	A7		♠	QJ98
♥			♥	AT753
♦	KQ9742		♦	853
♣	QJ974		♣	8

	♠	KT642
	♥	Q984
	♦	T
	♣	A63

	2♥	1N
type	44M	
scor	+110	+120
IMP	0	
MP	-1	

Tot IMP   +9

---- Tot MP ---

Win	Tie	Loss
4	0	1

Deal # 6

	♠	KJ
	♥	AQ2
	♦	K86
	♣	T7542

1N 2♣; then
2♦ 2♠; 3♣ 3♦

♠	AQ532		♠	86
♥	T54		♥	K8763
♦	Q7		♦	T43
♣	A98		♣	KJ6

	♠	T974
	♥	J9
	♦	AJ952
	♣	Q3

	3♦	1N
type	53m	
scor	-50	+90
IMP	-4	
MP	-1	

Tot IMP   +5

---- Tot MP ---

Win	Tie	Loss
4	0	2

		Deal #	7
♠	A65		
♥	A76	1N 2♣; then	
♦	K32	2♦ 2♠	
♣	QT85		

	2♠	1N

♠ KQ432		♠ 9			
♥ T4		♥ QJ952	type	43M	
♦ J64		♦ AQ	scor	-50	+90
♣ 763		♣ KJ942	IMP	-4	
			MP	-1	

♠	JT87	Tot IMP	+1
♥	K83		
♦	T9875	---- Tot MP ---	
♣	A		

Win	Tie	Loss
4	0	3

		Deal #	8
♠	K96		
♥	T8	1N 2♣; then	
♦	AK6	2♦ 2♥; 2♠	
♣	QJ943		

	2♠	1N

♠ AJT		♠ 874			
♥ J952		♥ AKQ	type	43M	
♦ Q4		♦ JT8532	scor	-50	+90
♣ 8765		♣ 2	IMP	-4	
			MP	-1	

♠	Q532	Tot IMP	-3
♥	7643		
♦	97	---- Tot MP ---	
♣	AKT		

Win	Tie	Loss
4	0	4

	♠	AKT8
	♥	AK2
	♦	T63
	♣	432

Deal # **9**

1N 2♣; then
2♠ 3♦

3♦	1N

♠	76542	♠	Q93
♥	QT	♥	8754
♦	KQ5	♦	J9
♣	KJ9	♣	AT65

type	53m	
scor	-50	+90
IMP	-4	
MP	-1	

	♠	J
	♥	J963
	♦	A8742
	♣	Q87

Tot IMP   -7

---- Tot MP ---

Win	Tie	Loss
4	0	5

	♠	KJ98
	♥	A94
	♦	93
	♣	AJ72

Deal # **10**

1N 2♣; then
2♠

2♠	1N

♠	642	♠	T7
♥	653	♥	KT8
♦	KQJ82	♦	AT76
♣	84	♣	KQT9

type	44M	
scor	+110	-50
IMP	+4	
MP	+1	

	♠	AQ53
	♥	QJ72
	♦	54
	♣	653

Tot IMP   -3

---- Tot MP ---

Win	Tie	Loss
5	0	5

		Deal #	**11**
♠	AJ98	1N 2♣; then	
♥	72	2♠	
♦	K82		
♣	A763		

	2♠	1N

♠ T3		♠ 752
♥ JT3		♥ KQ86
♦ QJ65		♦ AT94
♣ KJT4		♣ Q8

		2♠	1N
type	44M		
scor	-50		-50
IMP	0		
MP	0		

	♠	KQ64
	♥	A954
	♦	73
	♣	952

Tot IMP   -3

---- Tot MP ---

Win	Tie	Loss
5	1	5

		Deal #	**12**
♠	Q76	1N 2♣; then	
♥	Q3	2♦ 2♥; 2♠	
♦	J82		
♣	AK832		

	2♠	1N

♠ KT53		♠ AJ
♥ A2		♥ KT85
♦ 653		♦ Q97
♣ QJ94		♣ T765

		2♠	1N
type	43M		
scor	-50		-50
IMP	0		
MP	0		-3

	♠	9842
	♥	J9764
	♦	AKT4
	♣	

Tot IMP

---- Tot MP ---

Win	Tie	Loss
5	2	5

♠ K8
♥ K84
♦ KT42
♣ KQ95

Deal # **13**
1N 2♣; then
2♦ 2♥

	2♥	1N
type	53M	
scor	+110	+90
IMP	+1	
MP	+1	

♠ AT953   ♠ 72
♥ QJ7   ♥ 92
♦ 98753   ♦ AQJ
♣   ♣ A87632

♠ QJ64
♥ AT653
♦ 6
♣ JT4

Tot IMP   -2

---- Tot MP ---

Win	Tie	Loss
6	2	5

♠ AQJT8
♥ 964
♦ T5
♣ KQ4

Deal # **14**
1N 2♣; then
2♠

	2♠	1N
type	54M	
scor	+170	-50
IMP	+6	
MP	+1	

♠ K9   ♠ 54
♥ Q85   ♥ AT2
♦ AK92 ♦ QJ8743
♣ J632   ♣ 97

♠ 7632
♥ KJ73
♦ 6
♣ AT85

Tot IMP   +4

---- Tot MP ---

Win	Tie	Loss
7	2	5

♠ JT9	Deal # **15**
♥ KJT7	1N 2♣; then
♦ A6	2♥
♣ A872	

	2♥	1N

♠ AQ74	♠ K86	type	44M	
♥ 64	♥ Q83	scor	+170	+120
♦ T973	♦ J2	IMP	+2	
♣ KJ5	♣ QT964	MP	+1	

♠ 532	
♥ A952	Tot IMP +6
♦ KQ854	
♣ 3	---- Tot MP ---

Win	Tie	Loss
8	2	5

♠ 52	Deal # **16**
♥ AQ4	1N 2♣; then
♦ AJ854	2♦ 2♥
♣ Q97	

	2♥	1N

♠ 876	♠ Q93	type	43M	
♥ J95	♥ KT2	scor	+110	+120
♦ T92	♦ KQ7	IMP	0	
♣ A843	♣ KT62	MP	-1	

♠ AKJT4	
♥ 8763	Tot IMP +6
♦ 63	
♣ J5	---- Tot MP ---

Win	Tie	Loss
8	2	6

		♠	AQ94
		♥	KT63
		♦	J54
		♣	K4

Deal # **17**

1N 2♣; then

2♥

	2♥	1N

♠	T2	♠	763
♥	A82	♥	J5
♦	Q82	♦	AT93
♣	AQT95	♣	J732

type	44M	
scor	+170	+120
IMP	+2	
MP	+1	

	♠	KJ85
	♥	Q974
	♦	K76
	♣	86

Tot IMP   +8

---- Tot MP ---

Win	Tie	Loss
9	2	6

		♠	93
		♥	AJ832
		♦	K74
		♣	AQ2

Deal # **18**

1N 2♣; then

2♥

	2♥	1N

♠	KT2	♠	Q854
♥	K954	♥	7
♦	Q95	♦	AT
♣	JT5	♣	K98763

type	53M	
scor	+140	-50
IMP	+5	
MP	+1	

	♠	AJ76
	♥	QT6
	♦	J8632
	♣	4

Tot IMP   +13

---- Tot MP ---

Win	Tie	Loss
10	2	6

Deal # 19

	North
♠	AJT95
♥	K74
♦	A98
♣	Q9

West		East	
♠	864	♠	Q73
♥	JT8	♥	965
♦	J76	♦	KQ
♣	AJ82	♣	KT654

	South
♠	K2
♥	AQ32
♦	T5432
♣	73

1N 2♣; then
2♠ 3♦

	3♦	1N
type	53m	
scor	+110	+120
IMP	0	
MP	-1	

Tot IMP +13

---- Tot MP ---
Win	Tie	Loss
10	2	7

Deal # 20

	North
♠	AK94
♥	Q62
♦	84
♣	K973

West		East	
♠	T2	♠	Q853
♥	AT8	♥	K94
♦	KJ95	♦	73
♣	AT86	♣	QJ42

	South
♠	J76
♥	J753
♦	AQT62
♣	5

1N 2♣; then
2♠

	2♠	1N
type	43M	
scor	-100	-100
IMP	0	
MP	0	

Tot IMP +13

---- Tot MP ---
Win	Tie	Loss
10	3	7

♠ AQ9
♥ Q62
♦ T86
♣ AQ85

Deal # **21**
1N 2♣; then
2♦ 2♠ [might P]

	2♠	1N

♠ J732	♠ 65
♥ AKJ75	♥ 943
♦	♦ KQ72
♣ J973	♣ KT64

type	43M	
scor	+110	+90
IMP	+1	
MP	+1	

♠ KT84
♥ T8
♦ AJ9543
♣ 2

Tot IMP +14

---- Tot MP ---

Win	Tie	Loss
11	3	7

♠ AT86
♥ KQ86
♦ 97
♣ KT3

Deal # **22**
1N 2♣; then
2♥

	2♥	1N

♠ K4	♠ 632
♥ 32	♥ A75
♦ AQT83	♦ 652
♣ J754	♣ AQ62

type	44M	
scor	+110	-100
IMP	+5	
MP	+1	

♠ QJ97
♥ JT94
♦ KJ4
♣ 98

Tot IMP +19

---- Tot MP ---

Win	Tie	Loss
12	3	7

♠	Q97
♥	AK9
♦	K9542
♣	T9

Deal # **23**

1N 2♣; then

2♦ 2♥

	2♥	1N

♠	J862		♠	AK5
♥	JT87		♥	63
♦	6		♦	QJ
♣	A853		♣	QJ7642

type	43M	
scor	+110	-50
IMP	+4	
MP	+1	

♠	T43
♥	Q542
♦	AT873
♣	K

Tot IMP   +23

---- Tot MP ---

Win	Tie	Loss
13	3	7

♠	Q2
♥	KJ983
♦	QJ3
♣	KQ5

Deal # **24**

1N 2♣; then

2♥

	2♥	1N

♠	KJ943		♠	A87
♥	QT		♥	65
♦	98742		♦	AK65
♣	T		♣	J972

type	54M	
scor	+170	-50
IMP	+6	
MP	+1	

♠	T65
♥	A742
♦	T
♣	A8643

Tot IMP   +29

---- Tot MP ---

Win	Tie	Loss
14	3	7

	♠	K72	
	♥	AQ4	
	♦	854	
	♣	AJ73	

Deal # **25**

1N 2♣; then
2♦ 2♥

♠	A83	♠	Q65
♥	T76	♥	85
♦	QJ3	♦	K976
♣	6542	♣	KQ98

	2♥	1N
type	53M	
scor	+140	+120
IMP	+1	
MP	+1	

	♠	JT94
	♥	KJ932
	♦	AT2
	♣	T

Tot IMP   +30

---- Tot MP ---

Win	Tie	Loss
15	3	7

	♠	QT75
	♥	KT6
	♦	A862
	♣	A9

Deal # **26**

1N 2♣; then
2♠

♠	J842	♠	93
♥	J852	♥	A4
♦	4	♦	KQJ
♣	K753	♣	QJT862

	2♠	1N
type	43M	
scor	+140	+90
IMP	+2	
MP	+1	

	♠	AK6
	♥	Q973
	♦	T9753
	♣	4

Tot IMP   +32

---- Tot MP ---

Win	Tie	Loss
16	3	7

	♠	93
	♥	AK64
	♦	A74
	♣	J876

Deal # **27**

1N 2♣; then
2♥ 2♠; 2NT 3♦

♠	QJ752	♠	A4
♥	Q972	♥	T853
♦	8	♦	KJ32
♣	QT4	♣	A52

3♦	1N

type	53m	
scor	+110	+90
IMP	+1	
MP	+1	

	♠	KT86
	♥	J
	♦	QT985
	♣	K93

Tot IMP   +33

---- Tot MP ---

Win	Tie	Loss
17	3	7

	♠	A763
	♥	T6
	♦	AK9
	♣	QT92

Deal # **28**

1N 2♣; then
2♠

♠	8	♠	T952
♥	AK982	♥	Q4
♦	Q852	♦	T74
♣	K84	♣	A765

2♠	1N

type	44M	
scor	+110	+120
IMP	0	
MP	-1	

	♠	KQJ4
	♥	J753
	♦	J63
	♣	J3

Tot IMP   +33

---- Tot MP ---

Win	Tie	Loss
17	3	8

	♠	AKJ7
	♥	Q84
	♦	63
	♣	QJ63

Deal # **29**

1N 2♣; then
2♠

	2♠	1N
type	43M	
scor	+110	+120
IMP	0	
MP	-1	

♠ 532	♠ 984
♥ AT93	♥ 75
♦ 98	♦ AQJ4
♣ AT95	♣ K742

	♠	QT6
	♥	KJ62
	♦	KT752
	♣	8

Tot IMP   +33

---- Tot MP ---

Win	Tie	Loss
17	3	9

	♠	865
	♥	KQ92
	♦	AK62
	♣	T6

Deal # **30**

1N 2♣; then
2♥

	2♥	1N
type	44M	
scor	+140	+90
IMP	+2	
MP	+1	

♠ KQ4	♠ J932
♥ J854	♥ 6
♦ T753	♦ Q984
♣ AK	♣ QJ85

	♠	AT7
	♥	AT73
	♦	J
	♣	97432

Tot IMP   +35

---- Tot MP ---

Win	Tie	Loss
18	3	9

♠	AK3	
♥	Q432	
♦	K3	
♣	9853	

Deal # **31**

1N 2♣; then
2♥

	2♥	1N

	♠ JT54		♠ Q92
	♥ T76		♥ A9
	♦ 98		♦ QT2
	♣ AKJ6		♣ QT742

type	44M	
scor	+230	+90
IMP	+3	
MP	+1	

♠	876	
♥	KJ85	
♦	AJ7654	
♣		

Tot IMP   +38

---- Tot MP ---

Win	Tie	Loss
19	3	9

♠	AK	
♥	AQ3	
♦	J532	
♣	T965	

Deal # **32**

1N 2♣; then
2♦ 2♠; 2NT 3♣

	3♣	1N

	♠ QJ542		♠ 96
	♥ K9854		♥ JT76
	♦ Q87		♦ K96
	♣		♣ AJ82

type	54m	
scor	+130	+150
IMP	-1	
MP	-1	

♠	T873	
♥	2	
♦	AT4	
♣	KQ743	

Tot IMP   +37

---- Tot MP ---

Win	Tie	Loss
19	3	10

	♠	KJT97
	♥	A87
	♦	T6
	♣	AT7

Deal # **33**

1N 2♣; then
2♠

♠	64		♠	Q8
♥	QT643		♥	9
♦	KJ7		♦	AQ985
♣	Q43		♣	KJ865

	2♠	1N
type	54M	
scor	+140	+120
IMP	+1	
MP	+1	

	♠	A532
	♥	KJ52
	♦	432
	♣	92

Tot IMP   +38

---- Tot MP ---

Win	Tie	Loss
20	3	10

	♠	AQ85
	♥	73
	♦	AT875
	♣	K6

Deal # **34**

1N 2♣; then
2♠

♠	93		♠	T2
♥	KQ86		♥	942
♦	94		♦	KQJ2
♣	AQJ92		♣	7543

	2♠	1N
type	54M	
scor	+170	+120
IMP	+2	
MP	+1	

	♠	KJ764
	♥	AJT5
	♦	63
	♣	T8

Tot IMP   +40

---- Tot MP ---

Win	Tie	Loss
21	3	10

♠ KQ7	Deal # **35**
♥ J6	1N 2♣; then
♦ QJ76	2♦ 2♥; 2NT 3♣
♣ A954	

	3♣	1N

♠ AT987	♠ 6532
♥ 732	♥ AQ98
♦ KT95	♦ A43
♣ J6	♣ 32

	3♣	1N
type	54M	
scor	+110	+120
IMP	0	
MP	-1	

♠ J4
♥ KT54
♦ 82
♣ KQT87

Tot IMP   +40

---- Tot MP ---

Win	Tie	Loss
21	3	11

♠ AJ74	Deal # **36**
♥ AK93	1N 2♣; then
♦ 654	2♥
♣ T5	

	2♥	1N

♠ KT863	♠ Q95
♥ T76	♥ J5
♦ KJ3	♦ AQ987
♣ 98	♣ A72

	2♥	1N
type	44M	
scor	+170	-50
IMP	+6	
MP	+1	

♠ 2
♥ Q842
♦ T2
♣ KQJ643

Tot IMP   +46

---- Tot MP ---

Win	Tie	Loss
22	3	11

```
        ♠  AQ74
        ♥  Q96
        ♦  KJ64
        ♣  J2

♠  KJ853      ♠  T6
♥  T8         ♥  AK43
♦  92         ♦  Q8753
♣  KQ53       ♣  76

        ♠  92
        ♥  J752
        ♦  AT
        ♣  AT984
```

Deal # **37**

1N 2♣; then

2♠ 3♣

3♣	1N

type	52m	
scor	-50	+120
IMP	-5	
MP	-1	

Tot IMP   +41

---- Tot MP ---

Win	Tie	Loss
22	3	12

```
        ♠  K75
        ♥  A982
        ♦  AJ7
        ♣  T95

♠  Q94        ♠  J82
♥  J765       ♥  KQ4
♦  Q5         ♦  T62
♣  Q843       ♣  AK76

        ♠  AT63
        ♥  T3
        ♦  K9843
        ♣  J2
```

Deal # **38**

1N 2♣; then

2♥ 2♠

2♠	1N

type	43M	
scor	+140	+120
IMP	+1	
MP	+1	

Tot IMP   +42

---- Tot MP ---

Win	Tie	Loss
23	3	12

Deal # **39**

1N 2♣; then
2♠

	2♠	1N
type	44M	
scor	+110	-50
IMP	+4	
MP	+1	

```
          ♠ AK82
          ♥ KQ6
          ♦ T32
          ♣ Q73
♠ QJT75        ♠
♥ 9874         ♥ JT3
♦ A            ♦ Q875
♣ J42          ♣ AKT865
          ♠ 9643
          ♥ A52
          ♦ KJ964
          ♣ 9
```

Tot IMP   +46

---- Tot MP ---

Win	Tie	Loss
24	3	12

Deal # **40**

1N 2♣; then
2♦ 2♥; 2♠ 3♣

	3♣	1N
type	54m	
scor	+110	+90
IMP	+1	
MP	+1	

```
          ♠ AQ6
          ♥ JT
          ♦ Q862
          ♣ AJT9
♠ J753         ♠ KT9
♥ Q84          ♥ A976
♦ K953         ♦ AJ74
♣ 86           ♣ 54
          ♠ 842
          ♥ K532
          ♦ T
          ♣ KQ732
```

Tot IMP   +47

---- Tot MP ---

Win	Tie	Loss
25	3	12

Deal # 41

	♠	Q7
	♥	K74
	♦	T874
	♣	AQJ5

1N 2♣; then
2♦ 2♥

♠	KT62		♠	843
♥	QJ3		♥	AT8
♦	A93		♦	K652
♣	T93		♣	K42

	♠	AJ95
	♥	9652
	♦	QJ
	♣	876

	2♥	1N
type	43M	
scor	-100	-50
IMP	-2	
MP	-1	

Tot IMP   +45

---- Tot MP ---
Win	Tie	Loss
25	3	13

Deal # 42

	♠	A7
	♥	982
	♦	K765
	♣	KQJ4

1N 2♣; then
2♦ 2♥

♠	JT842		♠	3
♥	JT		♥	AK53
♦	AQ8		♦	T9432
♣	632		♣	A87

	♠	KQ965
	♥	Q764
	♦	J
	♣	T95

	2♥	1N
type	43M	
scor	-50	-50
IMP	0	
MP	0	

Tot IMP   +45

---- Tot MP ---
Win	Tie	Loss
25	4	13

♠ K2	Deal # **43**
♥ K952	1N 2♣; then
♦ AQ853	2♥
♣ 96	

	2♥	1N

♠ AJ94	♠ T8763
♥ 84	♥ AT7
♦ J92	♦ K64
♣ AQT4	♣ 52

	2♥	1N
type	44M	
scor	-50	-100
IMP	+2	
MP	+1	

♠ Q5
♥ QJ63
♦ T7
♣ KJ873

Tot IMP   +47

---- Tot MP ---

Win	Tie	Loss
26	4	13

♠ A543	Deal # **44**
♥ K986	1N 2♣; then
♦ 85	2♥
♣ AQJ	

	2♥	1N

♠ J862	♠ 7
♥ 75	♥ AQJ
♦ AKQJ7	♦ T6432
♣ 97	♣ 8632

	2♥	1N
type	44M	
scor	+140	-50
IMP	+5	
MP	+1	

♠ KQT9
♥ T432
♦ 9
♣ KT54

Tot IMP   +52

---- Tot MP ---

Win	Tie	Loss
27	4	13

	♠ T2		
	♥ T862		
	♦ AKQ2		
	♣ KJT		

Deal # **45**

1N 2♣; then

2♥

	2♥	1N

♠ KJ63		♠ 984
♥ 53		♥ AK4
♦ 8543		♦ J976
♣ Q63		♣ A98

type	44M	
scor	+140	+120
IMP	+1	
MP	+1	

	♠ AQ75
	♥ QJ97
	♦ T
	♣ 7542

Tot IMP   +53

---- Tot MP ---

Win	Tie	Loss
28	4	13

	♠ QJ85		
	♥ QT6		
	♦ Q97		
	♣ AK7		

Deal # **46**

1N 2♣; then

2♠

	2♠	1N

♠ A43		♠ KT
♥ K32		♥ 75
♦ K652		♦ JT84
♣ J85		♣ Q9632

type	44M	
scor	+140	+90
IMP	+2	
MP	+1	

	♠ 9762
	♥ AJ984
	♦ A3
	♣ T4

Tot IMP   +55

---- Tot MP ---

Win	Tie	Loss
29	4	13

Deal # 47

♠ 6542
♥ AK
♦ 95
♣ AQJ52

1N 2♣; then
2♠

	2♠	1N
type	54M	
scor	+200	+120
IMP	+2	
MP	+1	

♠ 93		♠ Q8
♥ 8532		♥ QJ4
♦ A72		♦ KQJ63
♣ K964		♣ T87

♠ AKJT7
♥ T976
♦ T84
♣ 3

Tot IMP   +57

---- Tot MP ---

Win	Tie	Loss
30	4	13

Deal # 48

♠ A72
♥ QJ965
♦ A52
♣ Q6

1N 2♣; then
2♥ 2♠

	2♠	1N
type	43M	
scor	+110	+90
IMP	+1	
MP	+1	

♠ 954		♠ Q83
♥ KT87		♥ A32
♦ KJ		♦ QT643
♣ J954		♣ K3

♠ KJT6
♥ 4
♦ 987
♣ AT872

Tot IMP   +58

---- Tot MP ---

Win	Tie	Loss
31	4	13

	♠	Q92
	♥	AK762
	♦	65
	♣	A87

Deal # **49**

1N 2♣; then
2♥

	2♥	1N

♠	KT864		♠	73
♥	T		♥	QJ9
♦	AQT3		♦	72
♣	T64		♣	KQJ932

		2♥	1N
type	54M		
scor	+140	-50
IMP	+5	
MP	+1	

	♠	AJ5
	♥	8543
	♦	KJ984
	♣	5

Tot IMP +63

---- Tot MP ---

Win	Tie	Loss
32	4	13

	♠	643
	♥	A97
	♦	QT72
	♣	AQJ

Deal # **50**

1N 2♣; then
2♦ 2♥

	2♥	1N

♠	Q92		♠	K85
♥	Q5		♥	K64
♦	AKJ65		♦	943
♣	T32		♣	9874

		2♥	1N
type	53M		
scor	+170	+150
IMP	+1	
MP	+1	

	♠	AJT7
	♥	JT832
	♦	8
	♣	K65

Tot IMP +64

---- Tot MP ---

Win	Tie	Loss
33	4	13

	♠	K7
	♥	J762
	♦	AT52
	♣	KQ7

Deal # **51**

1N 2♣; then
2♥

	2♥	1N
type	54M	
scor	+170	+120
IMP	+2	
MP	+1	

♠ A93	♠ 8542
♥ K5	♥ Q9
♦ Q98743	♦ K6
♣ 85	♣ AT632

	♠	QJT6
	♥	AT843
	♦	J
	♣	J94

Tot IMP   +66

---- Tot MP ---

Win	Tie	Loss
34	4	13

	♠	A83
	♥	Q96
	♦	AQJ96
	♣	J6

Deal # **52**

1N 2♣; then
2♦ 2♥

	2♥	1N
Type	43M	
Scor	+110	-50
IMP	+4	
MP	+1	

♠ J97	♠ QT6
♥ K84	♥ A72
♦ 42	♦ KT5
♣ KT752	♣ Q843

	♠	K542
	♥	JT53
	♦	873
	♣	A9

Tot IMP   +70

---- Tot MP ---

Win	Tie	Loss
35	4	13

			Deal #	**53**
♠	A62		1N 2♣; then	
♥	K9865		2♥	
♦	J6			
♣	AJ5			

	2♥	1N

♠ K9854	♠ Q3	
♥ 3	♥ QJ4	type
♦ KQT2	♦ 97	scor
♣ K74	♣ QT9632	IMP
		MP

	2♥	1N
type	54M	
scor	+170	+90
IMP	+2	
MP	+1	

♠	JT7
♥	AT72
♦	A8543
♣	8

Tot IMP   +72

---- Tot MP ---

Win	Tie	Loss
36	4	13

			Deal #	**54**
♠	KQ5		1N 2♣; then	
♥	85		2♦ 2♥; 2♠	
♦	A94			
♣	AT985			

	2♠	1N

♠ 4	♠ T876
♥ AJ964	♥ K3
♦ KT83	♦ Q765
♣ J42	♣ KQ7

	2♠	1N
type	53M	
scor	+110	+90
IMP	+1	
MP	+1	

♠	AJ932
♥	QT72
♦	J2
♣	63

Tot IMP   +73

---- Tot MP ---

Win	Tie	Loss
37	4	13

♠ QT87
♥ QJ64
♦ KQ9
♣ K9

Deal # **55**
1N 2♣; then
2♥

	2♥	1N

♠ KJ43
♥ 82
♦ 832
♣ QJ43

♠ A653
♥ AT3
♦ 76
♣ A752

type	44M	
scor	+140	+90
IMP	+2	
MP	+1	

♠ 3
♥ K975
♦ AJT54
♣ T86

Tot IMP   +75

---- Tot MP ---

Win	Tie	Loss
38	4	13

♠ 9853
♥ AK4
♦ JT7
♣ A93

Deal # **56**
1N 2♣; then
2♠

	2♠	1N

♠ K42
♥ Q63
♦ Q65
♣ QJ65

♠ Q6
♥ J95
♦ K82
♣ KT842

type	44M	
scor	+170	+90
IMP	+2	
MP	+1	

♠ AJT7
♥ T872
♦ A943
♣ 7

Tot IMP   +77

---- Tot MP ---

Win	Tie	Loss
39	4	13

	♠	JT5
	♥	Q32
	♦	AT42
	♣	AQT

Deal # **57**

1N 2♣; then
2♦ 2♥

	2♥	1N

♠	Q862	♠	A9
♥	T9	♥	A87
♦	K9865	♦	Q73
♣	63	♣	K8754

type	53M	
scor	+110	+90
IMP	+1	
MP	+1	

	♠	K743
	♥	KJ854
	♦	J
	♣	J92

Tot IMP   +78

---- Tot MP ---

Win	Tie	Loss
40	4	13

	♠	A53
	♥	KT75
	♦	T4
	♣	AQ94

Deal # **58**

1N 2♣; then
2♥

	2♥	1N

♠	KJT94	♠	Q762
♥	Q	♥	A842
♦	K65	♦	872
♣	JT85	♣	K7

type	44M	
scor	+140	+90
IMP	+2	
MP	+1	

	♠	8
	♥	J963
	♦	AQJ93
	♣	632

Tot IMP   +80

---- Tot MP ---

Win	Tie	Loss
41	4	13

	♠	J7542
	♥	KT3
	♦	AK2
	♣	K8

Deal # **59**

1N 2♣; then

2♠

♠	Q98	♠	3
♥	AJ4	♥	85
♦	J4	♦	Q9873
♣	A9752	♣	QJT43

	2♠	1N
type	54M	
scor	+170	+120
IMP	+2	
MP	+1	

	♠	AKT6
	♥	Q9762
	♦	T65
	♣	8

Tot IMP   +82

---- Tot MP ---

Win	Tie	Loss
42	4	13

	♠	A9742
	♥	74
	♦	AJT
	♣	KJ8

Deal # **60**

1N 2♣; then

2♠ 3♦

♠	JT83	♠	KQ65
♥	KQJ85	♥	62
♦	63	♦	54
♣	64	♣	AQ532

	3♦	1N
type	54m	
scor	+130	+120
IMP	0	
MP	+1	

	♠	
	♥	AT93
	♦	KQ9872
	♣	T97

Tot IMP   +82

---- Tot MP ---

Win	Tie	Loss
43	4	13

♠ T82
♥ AQ
♦ QJ6
♣ AJ983

Deal # **61**
1N 2♣; then
2♦ 2♥; 2♠

	2♠	1N
type	43M	
scor	-100	-50
IMP	-2	
MP	-1	

♠ K	♠ QJ954
♥ T973	♥ 54
♦ A753	♦ KT98
♣ KT72	♣ Q4

♠ A763
♥ KJ862
♦ 42
♣ 65

Tot IMP +80

---- Tot MP ---

Win	Tie	Loss
43	4	14

♠ KT76
♥ K865
♦ Q43
♣ KJ

Deal # **62**
1N 2♣; then
2♥

	2♥	1N
type	44M	
scor	-100	-50
IMP	-2	
MP	-1	

♠	♠ QJ942
♥ AJ72	♥ 3
♦ J9862	♦ AKT
♣ AT53	♣ 7642

♠ A853
♥ QT94
♦ 75
♣ Q98

Tot IMP +78

---- Tot MP ---

Win	Tie	Loss
43	4	15

	♠	J98
	♥	AQJ7
	♦	84
	♣	KJ53

Deal # **63**

1N 2♣; then
2♥

	2♥	1N

♠	7		♠	AKT43
♥	842		♥	93
♦	AKQJT3		♦	9752
♣	Q82		♣	T9

type	44M	
scor	+140	-50
IMP	+5	
MP	+1	

	♠	Q852
	♥	KT65
	♦	6
	♣	A764

Tot IMP +83

---- Tot MP ---

Win	Tie	Loss
44	4	15

	♠	KJ7
	♥	84
	♦	AQT85
	♣	KJ8

Deal # **64**

1N 2♣; then
2♦ 2♥; 2♠

	2♠	1N

♠	532		♠	986
♥	J93		♥	AKQ7
♦	K9		♦	643
♣	T9762		♣	A54

type	43M	
scor	+170	+120
IMP	+2	
MP	+1	

	♠	AQT4
	♥	T652
	♦	J72
	♣	Q3

Tot IMP +85

---- Tot MP ---

Win	Tie	Loss
45	4	15

Deal # 65

1N 2♣; then
2♠

```
            ♠ AT96
            ♥ QT4
            ♦ 98
            ♣ KQJ5

♠ J742          ♠ 5
♥ 65            ♥ AK7
♦ AQJ4          ♦ 7653
♣ 964           ♣ AT732

            ♠ KQ83
            ♥ J9832
            ♦ KT2
            ♣ 8
```

	2♠	1N
type	44M	
scor	-50	-50
IMP	0	
MP	0	

Tot IMP   +85

---- Tot MP ---

Win	Tie	Loss
45	5	15

Deal # 66

1N 2♣; then
2♥

```
            ♠ 964
            ♥ A765
            ♦ AKJ9
            ♣ J3

♠ JT53          ♠ KQ72
♥ 984           ♥ KJ
♦ T32           ♦ Q764
♣ AT2           ♣ Q86

            ♠ A8
            ♥ QT32
            ♦ 85
            ♣ K9754
```

	2♥	1N
type	44M	
scor	+140	+90
IMP	+2	
MP	+1	

Tot IMP   +87

---- Tot MP ---

Win	Tie	Loss
46	5	15

♠ A86	Deal # **67**
♥ K862	1N 2♣; then
♦ AJ	2♥ 2♠
♣ JT73	

	2♠	1N

♠ J9	♠ QT75
♥ AQ4	♥ J973
♦ T93	♦ Q86
♣ Q9542	♣ A8

	2♠	1N
type	43M	
scor	+140	+90
IMP	+2	
MP	+1	

♠ K432
♥ T5
♦ K7542
♣ K5

Tot IMP   +89

---- Tot MP ---

Win	Tie	Loss
47	5	15

♠ KQT	Deal # **68**
♥ Q98	1N 2♣; then
♦ KJ75	2♦ 2♥
♣ K64	

	2♥	1N

♠ 97542	♠ AJ6
♥ A72	♥ 654
♦ T83	♦ Q642
♣ A7	♣ Q95

	2♥	1N
type	43M	
scor	+140	+120
IMP	+1	
MP	+1	

♠ 83
♥ KJT3
♦ A9
♣ JT832

Tot IMP   +90

---- Tot MP ---

Win	Tie	Loss
48	5	15

♠	Q97
♥	A2
♦	T962
♣	AK32

Deal # 69

1N 2♣; then
2♦ 2♥; 2♠

2♠	1N

♠	K54		♠	AJ
♥	9863		♥	KT4
♦	KQ		♦	7543
♣	T765		♣	Q984

type	53M	
scor	+110	+90
IMP	+1	
MP	+1	

♠	T8632
♥	QJ75
♦	AK8
♣	J

Tot IMP   +91

---- Tot MP ---

Win	Tie	Loss
49	5	15

♠	K7
♥	952
♦	AT2
♣	AQJT6

Deal # 70

1N 2♣; then
2♦ 2♥

2♥	1N

♠	Q953		♠	T84
♥	KQJ7		♥	A8
♦	65		♦	Q943
♣	K32		♣	9875

type	43M	
scor	+140	+150
IMP	0	
MP	-1	

♠	AJ62
♥	T643
♦	KJ87
♣	4

Tot IMP   +91

---- Tot MP ---

Win	Tie	Loss
49	5	16

	♠ Q54		Deal # 71

♠ Q54
♥ A95
♦ T2
♣ AQJ96

Deal # **71**
1N 2♣; then
2♦ 2♥

	2♥	1N

♠ JT9	♠ 732
♥ K8	♥ Q62
♦ AJ5	♦ KQ843
♣ KT832	♣ 54

type	53M	
scor	+170	+90
IMP	+2	
MP	+1	

♠ AK86
♥ JT743
♦ 976
♣ 7

Tot IMP   +93

---- Tot MP ---

Win	Tie	Loss
50	5	16

♠ AJ532
♥ 972
♦ 74
♣ AKT

Deal # **72**
1N 2♣; then
2♠

	2♠	1N

♠ 6	♠ 987
♥ AKJ	♥ T83
♦ K852	♦ AQ93
♣ 98654	♣ QJ2

type	54M	
scor	+110	-50
IMP	+4	
MP	+1	

♠ KQT4
♥ Q654
♦ JT6
♣ 73

Tot IMP   +97

---- Tot MP ---

Win	Tie	Loss
51	5	16

♠ Q872
♥ A6
♦ A42
♣ QT76

Deal # **73**
1N 2♣; then
2♠

	2♠	1N
type	44M	
scor	-50	+90
IMP	-4	
MP	-1	

♠ 4   ♠ KJ96
♥ 43   ♥ KJT75
♦ J9863   ♦ KT7
♣ AK732   ♣ J

♠ A753
♥ Q982
♦ Q5
♣ 854

Tot IMP   +93

---- Tot MP ---

Win	Tie	Loss
51	5	17

♠ J7
♥ KQT87
♦ Q54
♣ A76

Deal # **74**
1N 2♣; then
2♥

	2♥	1N
type	54M	
scor	+170	-50
IMP	+6	
MP	+1	

♠ KQ64   ♠ AT32
♥ 2   ♥ 543
♦ 863   ♦ A9
♣ KQ982   ♣ JT54

♠ 985
♥ AJ96
♦ KJT72
♣ 3

Tot IMP   +99

---- Tot MP ---

Win	Tie	Loss
52	5	17

	♠	T8
	♥	AKJ8
	♦	QJ
	♣	J8765

Deal # **75**

1N 2♣; then
2♥

	2♥	1N
type	43M	
scor	-100	-150
IMP	+2	
MP	+1	

♠	A965		♠	KJ7
♥	96		♥	QT87
♦	A965		♦	T4
♣	T42		♣	AQ93

	♠	Q432
	♥	432
	♦	K8732
	♣	K

Tot IMP +101

---- Tot MP ---

Win	Tie	Loss
53	5	17

	♠	Q732
	♥	Q97
	♦	AK93
	♣	Q3

Deal # **76**

1N 2♣; then
2♠

	2♠	1N
type	44M	
scor	+140	+90
IMP	+2	
MP	+1	

♠	J8		♠	K96
♥	JT2		♥	A654
♦	JT874		♦	Q52
♣	AT2		♣	K86

	♠	AT54
	♥	K83
	♦	6
	♣	J9754

Tot IMP +103

---- Tot MP ---

Win	Tie	Loss
54	5	17

	♠ AJ63	
	♥ A8	
	♦ T87	
	♣ K974	

Deal # **77**
1N 2♣; then
2♠

♠ KT9		♠ 82
♥ 95		♥ KQJT6
♦ 942		♦ AJ653
♣ AQ862		♣ 3

	♠ Q754
	♥ 7432
	♦ KQ
	♣ JT5

	2♠	1N
type	44M	
scor	+110	-50
IMP	+4	
MP	+1	

Tot IMP +107

---- Tot MP ---

Win	Tie	Loss
55	5	17

	♠ A32	
	♥ QJ9	
	♦ KJ75	
	♣ KT7	

Deal # **78**
1N 2♣; then
2♦ 2♠

♠ J5		♠ KT87
♥ AT765		♥ K832
♦ T62		♦ 8
♣ AQ4		♣ 9853

	♠ Q964
	♥ 4
	♦ AQ943
	♣ J62

	2♠	1N
type	43M	
scor	+110	+120
IMP	0	
MP	-1	

Tot IMP +107

---- Tot MP ---

Win	Tie	Loss
55	5	18

♠ KQT5
♥ K54
♦ T5
♣ AQT5

Deal # **79**
1N 2♣; then
2♠

	2♠	1N

♠ 8	♠ A943	
♥ QJ93	♥ T8	type 44M
♦ KQ763	♦ AJ84	scor +140 +90
♣ 762	♣ 984	IMP +2
		MP +1

♠ J762
♥ A762
♦ 92
♣ KJ3

Tot IMP +109

---- Tot MP ---
Win	Tie	Loss
56	5	18

♠ 7652
♥ AK6
♦ K75
♣ K65

Deal # **80**
1N 2♣; then
2♠ 3♦

	3♦	1N

♠ AJ3	♠ T984	
♥ 9	♥ JT832	type 53m
♦ AQT8	♦ 4	scor -150 -100
♣ 98732	♣ AQJ	IMP -2
		MP 0

♠ KQ
♥ Q754
♦ J9632
♣ T4

Tot IMP +107

---- Tot MP ---
Win	Tie	Loss
56	5	19

102

	♠ A32		Deal # **81**	

♠ A32
♥ KQ83
♦ QT8
♣ JT3

Deal # **81**
1N 2♣; then
2♥

	2♥	1N

♠ KQJ5	♠ T64
♥ 42	♥ J76
♦ K762	♦ AJ954
♣ A75	♣ 64

type	44M	
scor	+140	-50
IMP	+5	
MP	+1	

♠ 987
♥ AT95
♦ 3
♣ KQ982

Tot IMP   +112

---- Tot MP ---

Win	Tie	Loss
57	5	19

♠ 98
♥ JT82
♦ AKJ8
♣ K95

Deal # **82**
1N 2♣; then
2♥

	2♥	1N

♠ KJT5	♠ A762
♥ Q53	♥ K7
♦ 5432	♦ Q976
♣ A2	♣ J76

type	44M	
scor	+110	+90
IMP	+1	
MP	+1	

♠ Q43
♥ A964
♦ T
♣ QT843

Tot IMP   +113

---- Tot MP ---

Win	Tie	Loss
58	5	19

♠ AK	Deal # **83**
♥ AJ843	1N 2♣; then
♦ Q62	2♥
♣ T76	

	2♥	1N

♠ 7532	♠ Q94
♥ T75	♥ Q
♦ 984	♦ AT53
♣ AKJ	♣ Q8532

type	44M	
scor	+170	+90
IMP	+2	
MP	+1	

♠ JT86
♥ K962
♦ KJ7
♣ 94

Tot IMP +115

---- Tot MP ---

Win	Tie	Loss
59	5	19

♠ AK52	Deal # **84**
♥ QJ7	1N 2♣; then
♦ 9864	2♠ 3♦
♣ A9	

	3♦	1N

♠ QJT8	♠ 764
♥ AT98	♥ 64
♦ J	♦ A52
♣ KJ86	♣ QT532

type	54m	
scor	+130	+90
IMP	+1	
MP	+1	

♠ 93
♥ K532
♦ KQT73
♣ 74

Tot IMP +116

---- Tot MP ---

Win	Tie	Loss
60	5	19

Deal # 85

	♠	Q975
	♥	KQ73
	♦	AQ6
	♣	83

♠ AKJ32	♠ 84
♥ AJ	♥ 542
♦ 9873	♦ KT52
♣ 64	♣ QT92

	♠	T6
	♥	T986
	♦	J4
	♣	AKJ75

1N 2♣; then
2♥

	2♥	1N
type	44M	
scor	+140	+120
IMP	+1	
MP	+1	

Tot IMP   +117

---- Tot MP ---

Win	Tie	Loss
61	5	19

Deal # 86

	♠	T7632
	♥	AQJ
	♦	Q63
	♣	AT

♠ Q	♠ K84
♥ 952	♥ KT6
♦ K975	♦ J842
♣ QJ842	♣ K97

	♠	AJ95
	♥	8743
	♦	AT
	♣	653

1N 2♣; then
2♠

	2♠	1N
type	54M	
scor	+140	+90
IMP	+2	
MP	+1	

Tot IMP   +119

---- Tot MP ---

Win	Tie	Loss
62	5	19

	♠ T2
	♥ AQT82
	♦ AT3
	♣ AT3

Deal # **87**

1N 2♣; then
2♥

♠ J83	♠ K76
♥ J5	♥ K7
♦ 986	♦ KQJ75
♣ Q8542	♣ J96

	2♥	1N
type	54M	
scor	+200	+120
IMP	+2	
MP	+1	

	♠ AQ954
	♥ 9543
	♦ 42
	♣ K7

Tot IMP +121

---- Tot MP ---

Win	Tie	Loss
63	5	19

	♠ QJ
	♥ Q85
	♦ T76
	♣ AKQ85

Deal # **88**

1N 2♣; then
2♦ 2♠; 3♣ 3♦

♠ A832	♠ 976
♥ KJ732	♥ A96
♦ 4	♦ AJ98
♣ T32	♣ J64

	3♦	1N
type	53m	
scor	-50	-50
IMP	0	
MP	0	

	♠ KT54
	♥ T4
	♦ KQ532
	♣ 97

Tot IMP +121

---- Tot MP ---

Win	Tie	Loss
63	6	19

	♠	AJ4
	♥	KJ
	♦	J874
	♣	Q653

Deal # **89**

1N 2♣; then
2♦ 2♥; 2♠

	2♠	1N

♠	T3		♠	8765
♥	AQ984		♥	T7
♦	5		♦	KQ92
♣	KJ742		♣	AT8

type	43M	
scor	+110	-50
IMP	+4	
MP	+1	

	♠	KQ92
	♥	6532
	♦	AT63
	♣	9

Tot IMP +125

---- Tot MP ---

Win	Tie	Loss
64	6	19

	♠	KQ854
	♥	J43
	♦	75
	♣	AK8

Deal # **90**

1N 2♣; then
2♠

	2♠	1N

♠	A		♠	JT2
♥	KQ5		♥	972
♦	AT843		♦	KJ2
♣	9764		♣	J532

type	54M	
scor	+110	-50
IMP	+4	
MP	+1	

	♠	9763
	♥	AT86
	♦	Q96
	♣	QT

Tot IMP +129

---- Tot MP ---

Win	Tie	Loss
65	6	19

♠ QT
♥ AQT2
♦ T5
♣ A8542

Deal # **91**

1N 2♣; then
2♥

	2♥	1N
type	44M	
scor	+110	-50
IMP	+4	
MP	+1	

♠ A532   ♠ KJ8
♥ J4   ♥ K86
♦ Q643   ♦ 987
♣ K63   ♣ QJT9

♠ 9764
♥ 9753
♦ AKJ2
♣ 7

Tot IMP   +133

---- Tot MP ---

Win	Tie	Loss
66	6	19

♠ AK3
♥ QT96
♦ Q43
♣ Q93

Deal # **92**

1N 2♣; then
2♥

	2♥	1N
type	44M	
scor	-100	-50
IMP	-2	
MP	-1	

♠ JT852   ♠ Q
♥ A83   ♥ 42
♦ 952   ♦ AJT87
♣ AT   ♣ K8752

♠ 9764
♥ KJ75
♦ K5
♣ J64

Tot IMP   +131

---- Tot MP ---

Win	Tie	Loss
66	6	20

	♠	AKQ7
	♥	Q4
	♦	K95
	♣	8632

Deal # **93**

1N 2♣; then
2♠

	2♠	1N

♠	J986		♠	4
♥	T87		♥	A652
♦	J8		♦	Q73
♣	K975		♣	AQJT4

type	44M	
scor	+200	+90
IMP	+3	
MP	+1	

♠	T532
♥	KJ93
♦	AT642
♣	

Tot IMP   +134

---- Tot MP ---

Win	Tie	Loss
67	6	20

	♠	A6
	♥	K9832
	♦	KT7
	♣	AT3

Deal # **94**

1N 2♣; then
2♥

	2♥	1N

♠	J98		♠	KT42
♥	AT74		♥	J
♦	J982		♦	A6543
♣	J9		♣	Q42

type	53M	
scor	+140	+120
IMP	+1	
MP	+1	

♠	Q753
♥	Q65
♦	Q
♣	K8765

Tot IMP   +135

---- Tot MP ---

Win	Tie	Loss
68	6	20

♠ A975
♥ K532
♦ A73
♣ QJ

Deal # **95**
1N 2♣; then
2♥ 2♠

	2♠	1N

♠ T62   ♠ K8
♥ AT76   ♥ QJ4
♦ JT52   ♦ 9864
♣ AK   ♣ 7532

type	44M	
scor	+140	+90
IMP	+2	
MP	+1	

♠ QJ43
♥ 98
♦ KQ
♣ T9864

Tot IMP   +137

---- Tot MP ---

Win	Tie	Loss
69	6	20

♠ T64
♥ AJ74
♦ J2
♣ AQ94

Deal # **96**
1N 2♣; then
2♥ 2♠

	2♠	1N

♠ AJ98   ♠ 75
♥ T65   ♥ Q832
♦ AT85   ♦ KQ943
♣ 82   ♣ K3

type	43M	
scor	-100	-50
IMP	-2	
MP	-1	

♠ KQ32
♥ K9
♦ 76
♣ JT765

Tot IMP   +135

---- Tot MP ---

Win	Tie	Loss
69	6	21

	♠	J92
	♥	A8
	♦	AKJ5
	♣	T864

Deal # **97**

1N 2♣; then
2♦ 2♥; 2♠

2♠	1N

♠	A3		♠	Q765
♥	QJ32		♥	K6
♦	Q9842		♦	73
♣	75		♣	KJ932

type	44M	
scor	+140	+150
IMP	0	
MP	-1	

	♠	KT84
	♥	T9754
	♦	T6
	♣	AQ

Tot IMP   +135

---- Tot MP ---

Win	Tie	Loss
69	6	22

	♠	QT8
	♥	A6
	♦	KJT7
	♣	QJ84

Deal # **98**

1N 2♣; then
2♦ 2♥; 2♠

2♠	1N

♠	2		♠	KJ965
♥	K8753		♥	T4
♦	98632		♦	A4
♣	K5		♣	A962

type	43M	
scor	-50	+90
IMP	-4	
MP	-1	

	♠	A743
	♥	QJ92
	♦	Q5
	♣	T73

Tot IMP   +131

---- Tot MP ---

Win	Tie	Loss
69	6	23

Deal # 99

	♠	J54
	♥	Q62
	♦	AK
	♣	KT873

1N 2♣; then
2♦ 2♠

♠	A3
♥	73
♦	Q943
♣	AJ642

♠	QJ86
♥	AJT84
♦	J5
♣	95

	♠	K972
	♥	K95
	♦	T8762
	♣	Q

	2♠	1N
type	43M	
scor	-50	-50
IMP	0	
MP	0	

Tot IMP +131

---- Tot MP ---

Win	Tie	Loss
69	7	23

Deal # 100

	♠	A8
	♥	AQ53
	♦	T42
	♣	A952

1N 2♣; then
2♥ 2♠; 3♦

♠	KQT
♥	JT864
♦	8
♣	JT86

♠	J765
♥	92
♦	AQJ6
♣	Q43

	♠	9432
	♥	K7
	♦	K9753
	♣	K7

	3♦	1N
type	53m	
scor	+130	+120
IMP	0	
MP	+1	

Tot IMP +131

---- Tot MP ---

Win	Tie	Loss
70	7	23

Match End

A major win for the scrambler! Matchpoint wins outnumber losses three to one (70 to 23)! These results are in line with our large *Landscape* studies. To summarize:

'Match' vs 'Landscape'
Scramble Contract Gains Over 1NT

	IMP	--- MP % ---		
	Gain	Win	Tie	Lose
'The 100 Match'	+1.3	70	7	23

Scramble contract makes 78%, 1NT 65%

'Landscape'	+1.3	65	9	26

Scramble contract makes 75%, 1NT 62%

The match results were slightly more favourable to the scramble contracts, compared to the much larger study, but totally within small-sample error margins.

Weakly qualifying hands, those (43)(42) holdings, are not reflected in either analysis.

The type of scramble contract was as follows, all within small-sample variance:

Contract Type	For '100 Match' %	For 'Landscape' %
43M	27	35
44M	36	32
53M	10	6
54+M	15	12
43-52m	1	3
44m	0	0
53m	7	7
54+m	4	5
Total	100	100

Appendix I --- Matchpoint Gains in Real Life

How do we map the matchpoint metric 'win/tie/lose' to actual matchpoint wins or losses at the club or tournament table? We've determined that scrambling translates to wins and losses approximately like this: *scramble contracts will win 65%, tie 9%, and lose 26%.* To simplify our analysis, we'll paint with a broad brush, and work with *wins outnumber losses by a two to one ratio.* It's actually closer to *two and one-half* to one, but we took the conservative road.

How do those results impact a real life matchpoint score? Here is a real-life example to illustrate the issue. You're pair #1, and you've played 1NT after opening 1NT with a five-card spade suit, missing your nice spade partial.

Contract	Pre-Scramble Score	MPs	Post-Scramble Score	MPs
1NT:2♠ N	+90	3.0	+170	10.0
3♠ N	+140	7.0	+140	6.0
2♣ E	-90	2.0	-90	2.0
3♠ N	+140	7.0	+140	6.0
3♠ N	-50	0.5	-50	0.5
2♠ N	+140	7.0	+140	6.0
3♠ N	+140	7.0	+140	6.0
3♠ N	+170	10.5	+170	10.0
2♠ N	+140	7.0	+140	6.0
2♠ N	+170	10.5	+170	10.0
4♠ N	-50	0.5	-50	0.5
3♣X E	+800	12.0	+800	12.0
2NT N	+120	4.0	+120	3.0

1NT scores poorly when a major suit fit is available. If you sit for it, you score 3.0 matchpoints. If you scramble as illustrated, your excellent declaring skills make 2♠ with two overtricks, scoring 10.0, a gain of 7.0. If instead you made just one overtrick in your scramble contract, you score 7.0 matchpoints for a gain of 4.0. Or say an unlucky lead holds you to eight tricks, your score remains at 3.0.

So your matchpoint gain depends largely on the context. What happened at the other tables? How large an improvement was the scramble score? How *diverse* are the scores? Those factors have huge variety, but we won't let that stop us from speculating generally.

We've approached this issue from a few perspectives.

Logic 101

You're a strong notrumper in a strong notrump field. On board X, everybody bids and makes 1NT, scoring 6.0 average. In another section, the informed, progressive guy playing Scramble Stayman scrambles to 2♠. Two-thirds of the time it makes, so he gets a top two-thirds of the time, and a bottom one-third. On average he scores 8.0 (2/3 x 12, less 1/3 x 0), a gain of 2.0 matchpoints.

Or you're a weak notrumper in a strong notrump field. You play in 1NT making, and everybody else is in 2♠ making. They score (close to) average, and you score 0.0. Had you trotted out Scramble Stayman, you too would score 6.0 two thirds of the time, and keep your bottom for the other third. Your average matchpoint gain in that scenario is about 4.0.

The Software Model

We built a model, and came to some conclusions. We're a weak notrumper in a strong notrump field. We're playing in 1NT and want to scramble into a better contract. We know those scramble contracts will be played by some of the rest of the field. That suggests our pre-scramble score is likely below average. Say on a 12.0 top and a 6.0 average, 1NT is currently scoring in the range of 3.0, give or take.

Given that context, a *win* for scrambling has a bigger upside than a *loss*. You can't do much worse than near-bottom. If your current score for 1NT is 3.0 (low, reflecting the fact you're outscored by a bunch of 2M contracts), your upside is up to 9.0 additional points, your downside just a couple of points.

In fact, our modelling shows that over a wide range of scenarios, the average matchpoint gain is about 4.5, and the average loss in the 1.2 range. With wins outnumbering losses two to one, that results in an average matchpoint pickup of about 2.6.

Real-life Example

We investigated a real-life club session of 26 boards and 13 players, and calculated every single matchpointing 'delta', defining delta as the difference between any two matchpoint scores. Say the matchpoint results on board one were these (we've sorted from top to bottom): 11.5 11.5 10.0 7.5 7.5 7.5 7.5 4.0 4.0 4.0 2.0 0.5 0.5.

The deltas, total differences in actual scores, are (11.5-10.0), (11.5-7.5) ... then (10-7.5) ... then more ... all the way down to (2.0-0.5).

For that board there are a total of fifteen deltas. The sum of the deltas is 82.5. The average delta is 5.5. We repeated that process for boards 2 through 26, and arrived at an overall average delta of 4.5.

That is to say the average 'distance' between any two matchpoint scores was 4.5. That I think is a not unreasonable proxy for what a typical gain from a scramble win or loss might be, and it aligns nicely with our modelling. With an average win = +4.5, and an average loss = -4.5, and a win/loss ration of two to one, the average net matchpoint gain is 1.5.

Here is another example. The deltas in the preceding table for the pre-scramble scores total 110, and average 5.2. That delta produces a net matchpoint gain of 1.7.

Summary

The question was 'what is the average matchpoint gain (loss) when you scramble to a higher-scoring (lower-scoring) contract'? This is not the most scientific thing we have ever done, but we have looked at this from several angles and arrived at 'not-unreasonable' estimates of 2.0, 4.0, 2.6, 1.5 and 1.7. *We feel safe in saying that the average net pickup is about 2.0 matchpoints.* Had we used a more realistic *two and one-half to one* ratio for wins to losses, that average pickup would be closer to 2.5 or 3.0.

There are other sources of gain, the two primary ones being these: (1) You will run into an occasional conditionally-invitational pickup, not otherwise possible. (2) The sequence (1NT) P (2♣) might deter or impede advancer, compared to (1NT) P (P).

Appendix II --- IMP Table

The International Match Point (IMP) Table:

Difference In Points	IMPs	Difference In Points	IMPs
20-40	1	750-890	13
50-80	2	900-1090	14
90-120	3	1100-1290	15
130-160	4	1300-1490	16
170-210	5	1500-1740	17
220-260	6	1750-1990	18
270-310	7	2000-2240	19
320-360	8	2250-2490	20
370-420	9	2500-2990	21
430-490	10	3000-3490	22
500-590	11	3500-3990	23
600-740	12	4000+	24

Appendix III --- Hand Distributions

Pattern	% of Hands
4432	21.6
4333	10.5
4441	3.0
5332	15.5
5431	12.9
5422	10.6
5521	3.2
5440	1.2
5530	0.9
6322	5.6
6421	4.7
6331	3.4
6430	1.3
6511	0.7
6521	0.7
6610	0.1
Others	4.1

CPSIA information can be obtained
at www.ICGtesting.com
Printed in the USA
FFOW01n1112120217
32225FF